Vegan Keto Diet:

The Ultimate Guide to Vegan Diet Plan and Prep: All You Need for Weight Loss in a Healthy Eating Regime to Reset and Energize Your Body and Mind with 50 Easy, Fast, and Delicious Recipes

By Brandon Pot

© Copyright 2020 - All rights reserved.

The content contained within this book may not be reproduced, duplicated or transmitted without direct written permission from the author or the publisher.

Under no circumstances will any blame or legal responsibility be held against the publisher, or author, for any damages, reparation, or monetary loss due to the information contained within this book. Either directly or indirectly.

Legal Notice:

This book is copyright protected. This book is only for personal use. You cannot amend, distribute, sell, use, quote or paraphrase any part, or the content within this book, without the consent of the author or publisher.

Disclaimer Notice:

Please note the information contained within this document is for educational and entertainment purposes only. All effort has been executed to present accurate, up to date, and reliable, complete information. No warranties of any kind are declared or implied. Readers acknowledge that the author is not engaging in the rendering of legal, financial, medical or professional advice. The content within this book has been derived from various sources. Please consult a licensed professional before attempting any techniques outlined in this book.

By reading this document, the reader agrees that under no circumstances is the author responsible for any losses, direct or indirect, which are incurred as a result of the use of information contained within this document, including, but not limited to, — errors, omissions, or inaccuracies.

Table of Contents

5. Cauliflower Hash Browns

6. Maple Oatmeal

7. Mediterranean Style Breakfast Burrito

8. Vegan Bagels

9. Quiche Cups

10. Chocolate Cinnamon Smoothie

Lunch Recipes

1. Mushroom Sandwich with Greens

2. Grilled Eggplant Rollups

3. Greek Salad

4. Peppers Stuffed with Vegetables

5. Spicy Lentil Soup

6. Tomato and Red Pepper Soup

7. Nicoise Salad

8. Cilantro Lime Coleslaw

9. Zucchini Noodles with Avocado Sauce

10. Cauliflower Fried Rice

11. Roast Baby Eggplant

12. Sweet Potato and Squash Patties

13. Cranberry Chickpea Salad

14. Thai Soup

15. Butternut Squash with Mustard Vinaigrette

Dinner Recipes

1. Zucchini Lasagna

2. Tofu in Tomatoes

3. Cauliflower Rice with Mushrooms

4. Spaghetti Squash Greek Style

5. Stuffed Portobello Mushrooms

6. Creamy Curry Noodles

7. Portobello Mushroom Tacos

8. Sushi Bowl

9. Egg Roll in a Bowl

10. Zucchini Ravioli

11. Indian Roasted Vegetables

12. Cauliflower Pie

13. Korean Beef Bowl

14. Veggie Salad Bowl

15. Roast Brussel Sprouts with Garlic and Red Pepper

Desserts

1. Spiced Chocolate

Introduction

Congratulations on purchasing *Vegan Keto Diet: The Ultimate Guide to Vegan Diet Plan and Prep: All You Need for Weight Loss in a Healthy Eating Regime to Reset and Energize Your Body and Mind with 50 Easy, Fast, and Delicious Recipes* by Brandon Pot and our thanks for choosing this book.

The following chapters will discuss in great detail the vegan version of the ketogenic, or keto, diet. This book will tell you everything that you need to know about following the keto diet with vegan foods and recipes. It will be explained in great detail exactly what the keto vegan diet is, how it will benefit you, and how easy it will be to reach your health and wellness goals while following this diet.

The vegan diet is not new, and neither is the keto diet, although both have enjoyed a renewed popularity in recent years because they work. Our ancestors lived on plants for centuries, and pretty much lived a vegan keto lifestyle without knowing they were doing it. To them, it was just their way of life. And this book will give you everything that you need to know to make it your way of life.

You will learn what food options are available to you and how to put foods together to make a nutritious meal plan. You will see how easy it is to make your food taste good when you learn to use herbs and spices. Being able to balance your food groups in the right way to benefit your body and help you to reach your goals is important, and there will be information to get you started on the right track. And there will be delicious recipes for every meal of the day plus a few for dessert, to give you solid ideas on how easy it is to follow this vegan keto diet.

This is an exciting new journey for you, and we are glad that you chose this book to guide you along your new path to health and happiness.

Chapter 1: What Is a Keto Diet and How Does It Work

The keto diet is basically a diet that is high in fats. Your daily meals will include seventy to seventy-five percent fat, around five percent in carbohydrates (carbs), and the remainder will be made up of protein. Following the keto diet will allow your body to change from burning glucose, which your body gets from the food you eat, mainly carbs, to burning ketones, which come from fat metabolization, for the energy that your body needs. When you make the switch from relying on glucose to relying on ketones, you will find that your appetite decreases, your metabolism works faster, your muscles are stronger, and your risk of developing certain diseases is lessened.

When your body is treated the right way, it is an efficient little machine. Your body has the ability to switch itself from depending on carbs in times when food was plentiful to depending on fat for energy when food supplies were scarce. In ancient times when people were nomads, they would eat what they gathered when they found it. The idea was to eat while the food was available. This would often mean overeating, and the excess food would be stored as fat. The fat would be worked off during lean times when the body would turn to that stored fat to burn for fuel, and the person would become lean again.

But it was not until the twentieth century that the keto diet came under scrutiny by scientists and doctors. In studying ancient writings, they discovered that Greek physicians recommended strict dietary therapy as a cure for various illnesses and diseases. These researchers were intrigued by this idea, especially in the descriptions of using dietary therapy to cure people of 'the fits' which they deduced was an ancient term for epilepsy. Their theory was that it would be possible to alleviate the seizures, if not eliminate them completely, by using diet on people who had epilepsy. At that time, no medication existed to relieve people of their seizures, and many people found it impossible to live a full, complete life because of the seizures.

The first study had people consuming a vegetarian diet that was low in calories. The patients who adhered strictly to the diet were able to lessen the occurrence of their seizures and, in some cases, eliminate them completely. In studying these patients, the doctors were able to isolate three specific compounds that were found in the livers of people who were following the strict diet. They were named ketones, which is a word derived from an old German word for acetone. One of the chemical processes the ketones go through releases acetone, which can be detected on the breath of people following the diet.

Continued research led doctors to begin experimenting with the nutritional ratios of the diet to see if different results could be gained with different combinations of carbs, fats, and proteins. The standard formula that was used for many years was for the patient to consume no more than one gram of protein-based food for every pound that they weighed, no more than twenty grams of carbs each day, and the remainder of their daily diet would be made up from dietary fats. Other than the calculation for the protein intake that was-based on the patient's weight and keeping the carb count low, no other calculations were needed because calories were not restricted and did not need to be counted. As patients began to settle in and become accustomed to the diet, their seizures either lessened greatly in their frequency or stopped completely.

They also noticed that they were more alert and slept better than they ever had before.

The keto diet was the diet of choice for patients with epilepsy until the latter part of the twentieth century when prescription drugs for epilepsy became popular and more readily available. The anticonvulsant drugs were soon much more popular than the diet because of their convenience and lack of restrictions. Patients found it much easier to swallow a few pills than it was to adhere to a strict diet. The keto diet eventually became nothing more than an interesting note in historical references.

All of that changed in the 1990s when the keto diet once again became wildly popular. At that time, a producer and his wife were frantically searching for something to help their young son, who suffered from constant seizures that no medicine would alleviate. They stumbled across the keto diet in their research and decided to try it because, after all, nothing else had worked, and it certainly couldn't hurt their son. Almost immediately, his seizures lessened and then ceased completely. They told everyone they knew about the diet and even created a television documentary detailing their success. The keto diet was once again thrown into the spotlight.

During normal processes of metabolism, your body will burn carbs for fuel and energy. During digestion, your body will take these carbs and turn them into glucose (sugar) to be used throughout your body. Whenever you consume food, your brain sends a signal to your pancreas to begin secreting more of the hormone insulin. After the body has turned the digested food into glucose, the insulin hormone takes the glucose to your cells for energy. Under normal functioning, the pancreas will only secrete the amount of insulin that is needed to process the food that has just been eaten. When the glucose is produced, before it is transported by the insulin to the cells, an amount is stored in your liver that is large enough to fuel your body for about two days in the event you are facing a famine situation. This stored glucose is called glycogen.

People who eat a diet that is high in processed foods and sugary foods will have too much sugar in their bloodstream. These foods are easily broken down into glucose because they are carbs, and carbs easily turn to sugar in your body. Every time food is eaten, the brain sends out the signal for the pancreas to produce insulin until, eventually, the cells stop responding to the insulin because they have no more room to store glucose. Then the excess glucose is stored as fat, beginning around the organs of the midsection and spreading through the body as needed. When the cells begin to ignore the call of the insulin, this is known as insulin resistance. When the excess fat is stored around your midsection because your cells have no more room to store glucose, this is the beginning of metabolic syndrome. This condition can be corrected by adhering to the keto diet.

When you begin to restrict your intake of calories, your body knows it needs to find a new source of energy. It will look first to the glycogen that is stored in your liver. Once it has depleted that supply, it will turn to your stored fat to metabolize it to make fuel for the cells. The process for using the stored fat for energy releases the three acetone-based compounds that are known as ketone bodies or ketones. When this begins to happen, your body has reached a state of ketosis.

It can take anywhere from three days to one week for your body to enter into a state of ketosis. It must first use the two day supply of glycogen in the liver before it turns to your stored fat. The first major concern of the keto diet is to get your body into a state of ketosis so that it will start burning fat more efficiently. This ketosis is often referred to as nutritional ketosis because it is caused by your diet. Do not assume that ketosis is the same as ketoacidosis. The latter is a dangerous condition that affects people with diabetes.

Although some people sail right through the beginning of ketosis without any symptoms, most will experience what is known as the keto flu. It is called this because the early symptoms your exhibits when you enter ketosis may feel much like you have the flu. Some of the symptoms of your body going into ketosis that you might experience are these:

- Bad breath

- Bloating

- Constipation

- Headaches

- Increased food cravings, especially for carbs and sugary snacks

- Irritability or moodiness

- Muscle weakness during and after exercising

- Periods of fatigue and exhaustion

- Sleep disturbances

The bad breath that you may suffer during ketosis comes from your body releasing waste products. Your body has three ways in which it can release waste: through bathroom functions, through sweating, and through exhaling through the lungs and mouth. It really won't matter how many times you brush your teeth is your body is releasing toxins because brushing will not help your breath. Sucking on a sugar-free mint or chewing some sugar-free gum will usually take care of the problem, and it does not last for more than a few days.

There is more than one reason why you might begin to feel moody and irritable when you first start on the keto diet. When you eat carbs, they almost immediately turn into sugar in your body. It does not matter if the carb that you just ate is a sweet roll or a bowl of potatoes; to your body, a carb is a carb. So when you consume carbs, along with the insulin hormone, your brain will also signal your body to release two chemicals known as dopamine and serotonin. Dopamine is one of the transmitters that your body uses to send signals from the brain to the body and back through your nerves. Serotonin is often referred to as the happy hormone because it raises your feelings of happiness and wellbeing. So when you eat a cinnamon bun, the dopamine takes the serotonin through your body and your brain, and you feel happy. It is quite normal for your body to feel unhappy, or moody and irritable when you take the carbs away. As your body learns to rely on carbs less, then these feelings will subside.

And reducing the number of carbs you take in will lead to headaches, especially in the first two weeks on the diet. This is due to the imbalances in the electrolytes in your body. This is also responsible for the bloating, as the fat that is stored in your body holds water, and while you are trying to remove the fat, it is trying to hold on to more water. Just stay well hydrated because this will help you to flush out the excess toxins that are making you feel bloated and giving you headaches.

You may find it difficult to stick to an exercise routine, or any other kind of routine, in the first few weeks of the diet. As your body is getting used to using fat for energy, you will feel fatigued, lethargic, and sometimes totally exhausted. Your muscles may ache from the lack of energy as your body makes the change from glucose energy to ketone energy. During this time, you might want to keep your exercise routine focused on easy activities like walking or bicycling. The muscle fatigue will also be helped by staying well hydrated. You might also want to add a bit of sea salt and lemon juice to your water to add back in electrolytes you may be flushing out.

No matter how well you may be eating, you will probably suffer from food cravings. This is perfectly natural. There are now foods that you will not be eating, and it is natural to mourn their loss or want to cheat a bit and have some. That is why it is so important to get a full range of nutrition on the keto diet, and that includes eating the occasional keto-friendly dessert. And missing these foods you are craving, along with the loss of carbs, can interrupt your normal sleep patterns. This is another thing that sticking to a program of gentle exercise will assist with.

And while some people might experience absolutely no digestive upsets at all, others might experience diarrhea or constipation or maybe even both. Be sure to stay well hydrated and eating the right kinds of fiber-rich foods, and these digestive upsets will soon stop.

Getting used to the keto diet will take you a little time, but the benefits are well worth the effort you spend and any discomfort you might feel in the beginning.

Chapter 2: The Advantages of the Keto Diet

While the keto diet was originally developed to eliminate seizures in people with epilepsy, it has proven over and over again to have benefits that reach far past seizure control. Following the keto diet can help to prevent or eliminate many chronic health problems such as:

- Insulin resistance

- Metabolic syndrome

- Obesity

- Type 2 Diabetes

- Osteoarthritis

- Cardiovascular disease

- Certain types of cancers

- Inflammation

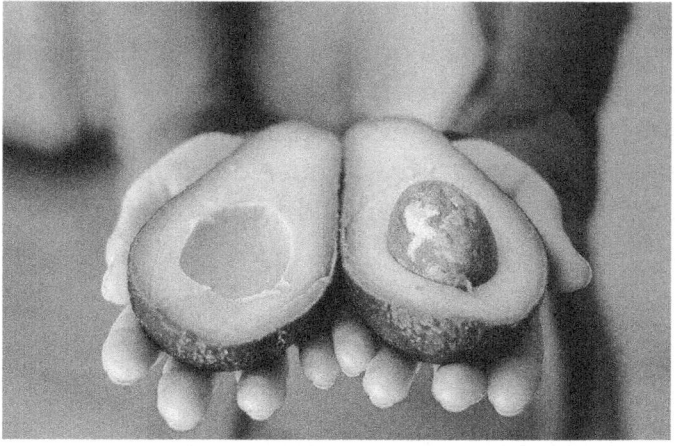

When you consume food, your body will produce insulin to help disperse the glucose from the food you just ate throughout the cells of your body. Metabolic syndrome happens when your cells stop responding to the insulin, and your body begins to store the excess fat. Once this begins to happen, then obesity is the next step. When you begin to follow the keto lifestyle, you will stop eating the carbs that immediately turn into sugar in your body, and you will begin to eat the fats that will make your body extract energy from the food that you eat. Your cells will once again answer the call when the insulin comes around. The excess weight on your body will begin to disappear as your body begins to use it for energy. The high-fat, moderate protein content will keep you feeling fuller longer, so there will be little to no temptation for you to overeat. You will begin to lose weight naturally.

When your weight begins to drop, and there is less glucose streaming through your bloodstream, then you will be helping to prevent the possibility of developing Type 2 Diabetes or reversing it if you already have it. As part of following the keto diet, you will be consuming little to no sugars since sugar will do nothing good for you once it is consumed. And since you will not be straining the pancreas to produce too much insulin and your cells will once again respond to the insulin your body produces, then there is a good possibility that you will be able to prevent the development of Type 2 Diabetes or reverse its effects if you already have developed it. Obesity is the number one factor in the development of Type 2 Diabetes.

As you eat and as you get hungry during the day, your blood sugar will naturally rise and fall. The problem comes when you are used to eating too much food or too many sugary and processed foods. When this happens, and your body is unable to process the constant flow of glucose in your blood, then your blood sugar level will be higher than it needs to be. This table shows what is considered to be normal blood sugar and at what level you are considered to have diabetes.

	FASTING	JUST ATE	3 HRS AFTER EATING
NORMAL	80 - 100	170 - 200	120 - 140
PRE-DIABETES	101 - 125	190 - 230	140 - 160
DIABETES	126 +	223 - 300	200 +

Being obese has a negative effect on your cardiovascular system. The cardiovascular system includes all the parts of your body that pertain to your heart and lungs, such as your arteries, heart, lungs, and veins. One of the measurements of the health of your cardiovascular system is your blood pressure reading. Your blood pressure is measured by looking at two numbers. The top number, or your systolic blood pressure, shows how much pressure that your blood exerts on the walls of the arteries when your heart is beating. The bottom number, your diastolic reading, shows how much pressure that your blood is putting on the walls of the arteries when your heart is at rest between beats.

	SYSTOLIC		DIASTOLIC
NORMAL	Less than 120	and	Less than 80
ELEVATED	120 - 129	and	Less than 80
HIGH BLOOD PRESSURE	130 - 179	and	90 - 120
HBP CRISIS LEVEL	180 and over	and /or	120 and over

Generally, more attention is given to the top reading because it is a direct indication of the health of your heart. However, if either number is elevated beyond a certain point and stays elevated for too long, then you have high blood pressure. Many different factors can affect your blood pressure. When people are obese, their bodies will create extra lengths of arteries to bring oxygen and nutrients to all the cells of the body. If the heart needs to pump harder to drive the blood through these extra arteries that could cause your blood pressure to be higher than normal. Also, as extra pressure is put on the walls of the arteries, they sometimes develop thin spots. Calcium deposits, waste products, and loose blood cells will collect in these weak spots and form deposits that are known as plaque. These deposits will eventually clog the artery so that the heart will need to work harder to push the blood through. If part of this plaque deposit breaks off and goes to your heart, it can cause you to have a heart attack. If the piece of plaque breaks off and goes to your brain, it can cause you to have a stroke.

Too much weight will also cause your lungs to need to work harder. Simply being overweight will make it harder for you to breathe well, and if there is a buildup of excess weight under and around your lungs, they will not be able to expand enough to allow you to bring in enough oxygen to supply the needs of your body. Excess weight will also put extra pressure on the joints in your lower body, causing them to wear out faster than normal and leading to osteoarthritis. And being overweight, and eating too much of the wrong type of food like processed foods and sugary snacks, will cause inflammation to develop in your body. And following the keto diet may help to prevent certain types of cancer or to help eliminate it if you already have it. Cancer cells are well fed with a sugary, processed foods diet, but they tend to starve when they are subjected to the typical high fat keto diet.

Your body will quickly adapt to the keto diet and will begin providing you all of the benefits of the keto diet. The carbs that you have been used to eating are the fuel source that your body prefers because it is the easiest source for your body to use. When you restrict your intake of carbs, your body reacts as though its food source had been cut off. It scrambles to find a new food source, and the only one available is the excess fat that your body has been storing. Changing to the keto diet is a big adjustment for your life and your body, so it takes your time getting used to it and be prepared to reap all of the rewards the diet has to offer.

Chapter 3: The Keto Vegan Diet

The vegan diet is the strictest version of all of the plant-based diets because it does not allow the consumption of any type of animal product, either those that are animals like meat and fish or those that come from animals like eggs and cheese. The vegan diet is based on plants only. Adhering to a vegan diet requires diligence because many canned or frozen foods that are plant-based will contain ingredients that are not plant-based. For example, unless you specifically look for vegan refried beans, you could be buying a version that contains lard, which is made from animal fat. Some foods might contain butter or margarine. And any food that is made with gelatin, which is made from the hooves and bones of animals, will be off-limits. Your diet will be built around vegetables, fruits, whole grains, seeds, nuts, legumes, and leafy greens.

While most people consider a vegan diet to be a vegan diet, there are actually several variations that you might choose to follow as you begin your new journey to a keto vegan lifestyle:

The Whole Food Vegan Diet: On this diet, you will eat a variety of whole plant foods such as whole grains, veggies, fruits, seeds, nuts, and legumes. This is the typical vegan diet that most people think of when they think of following a vegan diet.

The Starch Solution: On this vegan diet, you will focus on eating mostly corn, rice, and potatoes. This version would not work with the keto diet because of its high carb content.

The 80/10/10 Plan: On this vegan version, you will eat limited amounts of plants that are rich in plant fats like avocadoes and nuts, and you will rely mostly on leafy greens and raw fruits to make your meals. This plan also would not work with the keto diet because of the high fruit content and the limited amounts of plant fat.

The Raw Food Vegan Diet: On this version, you will eat a whole food plant-based diet, but most of the food that you eat will be raw. Anything that is cooked must be cooked at a temperature no higher than one hundred eighteen degrees, which eliminates almost every form of cooking except steaming.

The Raw until Four Plan: This plan could work with the keto diet because it mandates only raw foods eaten until four in the afternoon, and then you have the option of consuming a cooked meal for the evening.

The Junk Food Vegan Diet: Some people might be fooled into thinking that this option could work on the keto diet because it allows you to eat meats and cheeses that have been made from plants, but those items are usually high in carbs and proteins and generally low in fats. To make this option to work on the keto diet, you will need to read every food label carefully.

The vegan diet has many of the same health benefits as the keto diet does. The higher fiber intake of the vegan diet can help you to lose weight even if you eat until you are full and don't count calories. With weight loss, you may have a reduction in the blood glucose that can lead to a diagnosis of Type 2 Diabetes. Your joints will have less pressure on them, and your inflammation will be lessened, if not disappear completely. You may also prevent the onset of cardiovascular disease and certain cancers.

The vegan keto diet is simply a plant-based version of the keto diet. On the vegan keto diet plan, you will get most of your energy needs from protein and fats. Since the vegan diet does not rely on animal products, they are usually higher in carbs than the traditional keto diet. It will be more challenging to follow a keto diet if you are following a vegan diet. Careful planning will allow you to make appropriate menus. Only plant-based food is allowed, and carb intake is restricted significantly. The diet does not include any products made from animals, but it is high in fats and does contain an amount of protein that is adequate for good health.

When you are planning your meals, you will need to pay special attention to your macronutrients. A macronutrient is a compound that is eaten in large quantities to give you the bulk of energy that you need to fuel your body. The three macronutrients (macros) in your food are proteins, fats, and carbohydrates. The macros ratios for the vegan keto diet are slightly different than they are for a regular keto diet because the fat ratio is a bit lower. The standard keto diet fat ratio is seventy to seventy-five percent of your daily caloric consumption. On the vegan keto diet, the fats requirement is fifty-five to sixty percent of your daily calories. You can always make your percentage of fat higher if you like. The remainder of the calories is divided between protein at thirty to thirty-five percent and carbs at five to ten percent. With this carb macro, a person on a two thousand calorie a day diet will eat just twenty-five to fifty grams of carbs per day. Assuming that you are consuming a diet that is sixty percent fat, thirty-five percent protein, and five percent carbs, this is what the macro breakdown would look like for various calorie counts.

DAILY TOTAL CALORIE COUNT	FATS	PROTEIN	CARBS
2000	1200	700	100
1800	1080	630	90
1500	900	525	75
1200	720	420	60
1000	600	350	50

When you are calculating grams of food for your meal plans, keep in mind that one gram of carbs or protein will equal four calories. Since fat has more than twice the number of calories that carbs and protein do, one gram of fat has nine calories. Keeping to the same calorie counts as the previous chart, this chart shows how many grams of each macro would be consumed for each daily total calorie count.

DAILY TOTAL CALORIE COUNT	FATS GRAMS	PROTEIN GRAMS	CARBS GRAMS
2000	133	175	25
1800	120	158	22
1500	100	132	19
1200	80	105	15
1000	67	88	13

While it seems to be difficult to restrict the intake of carbs on a regular keto diet, it can seem to be quite impossible on a vegan keto diet. Part of the consideration you must pay attention to on the vegan keto diet is getting enough fats and proteins without eating too many carbs and knocking yourself out of ketosis.

It is very possible to do keto on a vegan diet, but it will require dealing with a specific set of challenges. If you are following a plant-based keto diet, you will need to focus on low starch veggies as well as veggies that are high in their content of fat. You will also concentrate on berries, seeds, nuts, and oil. There are alternative vegan foods available on the market that can provide fat and protein while keeping their vegan label, such as vegan burgers, vegan cheese, and vegan mayonnaise. The key to using them is to read the labels carefully to prevent eating too many carbs or eating any food that has added sugar.

If you plan to use processed vegan foods, like the ones that are consumed on the Junk Food Vegan Diet, you will need to understand what you are reading on the food label. When you are reading a food label, and you see the words "Total Carbs" which is the sum of the carbs, sugars, and dietary fiber in that serving of food. All sugars will be classified as carbs even though not every carb is a sugar.

You will find that "dietary fiber" is the first item that is listed under the category of Total Carbs. The values that are provided are usually the weight of the dietary fiber in grams and the percent of the total intake for someone who is following a two thousand calorie a day diet. The fiber that you consume is counted as part of your total carbs, but it is not part of your net carbs, and net carbs are the number that you need to count on your low carb diet. Your body is not able to digest fiber, and since it passes right through you, it is not counted in your carb count.

You also need to know the sugar content of your foods. Whether it is an ingredient naturally because one of the food ingredients has sugar content or sugar was added to the finished product, sugar in all forms is forbidden on the vegan keto diet. Some of the more widely used label names for sugar and added sugar that you will see on a food label are glucose, lactose, sucrose, fructose, dextrose, maltose, galactose, brown sugar, beet sugar, cane sugar, confectioner's sugar, corn syrup, corn syrup solids, dextrin, golden sugar, maltodextrin, agave, molasses, caramel, and high fructose corn syrup. And those are only about half of the different ways that sugar can be listed on a food label.

Also, look at the number of servings. Do not automatically assume that because the package is small, the entire package is one serving. Pay attention to the saturated fats, as those are the ones that are bad for you. And also pay attention to how many proteins are in the serving.

With some good planning, you will easily be able to make meals out of vegan food items and still stay true to the idea of the keto diet.

Chapter 4: Foods of the Keto Vegan Diet

Following a keto diet and eating as a vegan requires careful planning, but it can be done. One consideration is the fact that humans need to consume complete proteins that contain all nine of the amino acids that are considered essential for the human body to function properly. These are considered to be essential nutrients because they are necessary for life, but the human body can't manufacture them. They must be found in the dietary choices. Proteins that come from animals will provide all of the essential amino acids that you need in the amounts that you need, but the plants you eat only contain some of the essential amino acids.

Eating both vegan and low carb might sound strange together at first. Low carb or keto diets always include animal products that will provide you with an adequate supply of fats while keeping carbs to a minimum. Vegan diets do not contain any animal products and are usually high in carbs while they are low in fat, which is the exact opposite breakdown of what is required on the keto diet.

It is possible to eat a low carb keto diet while still staying true to your vegan lifestyle. One of the benefits that you will experience is that you will be hungry less often, which will enable you to lose more weight. Other benefits of low carb eating are reduction of high blood pressure, elimination of insulin resistance, better control of diabetes, and lowered levels of inflammation.

A vegan diet that is well planned and-based on healthy whole plant foods will provide enough protein needed for your daily intake. And while it will not provide all of the minerals and vitamins that your body requires, it will provide most of them. The hardest thing you will find to do on the vegan keto diet is meeting all of the nutritional needs that are essential for keeping your body strong and healthy. Here are five definite must-dos to keep in mind when you are implementing your vegan keto diet.

1. Don't forget to take supplemental vitamins if needed. You can meet most of your essential nutritional needs when you are following a vegan diet. Supplementing your diet with vitamin B-12 might be necessary because that particular vitamin is only found in animal foods. Unless you plan to eat vitamin B-12 fortified foods or take supplements, you are at a really high risk of being deficient in this vitamin. If you do not take supplements of this vitamin, then you will be at risk of some serious, possibly irreversible medical issues like dementia, nerve damage, and anemia. It is not difficult to locate vitamin B-12 supplements that are vegan-friendly.

2. Choose menu items from plants that are full of nutrients. The vegan proteins that you eat will provide some of the carbs that you will need. The remainder of the carbs in your daily diet should be sourced from vegetables that are grown above the ground, certain berries, seeds, and nuts. Besides providing you with good dietary fiber, these plant-based foods will provide you with the necessary minerals and vitamins. And when they are consumed along with healthy fats, they will taste absolutely delicious.

3. Always make it a point to include fats that are healthy in your meal plans. The fat macro will give you most of the calories that you will consume daily while you are following the vegan keto diet. You will be consuming a high-fat, low carb vegan diet. While there are guidelines for the fat macro that you should not fall below, there are no strict limits like there are with carbs and proteins. As long as you are consuming the minimum amount of fats on your diet, feel free to go over that amount because the fat content of the foods that you eat is what will make you feel full and keep you feeling fuller longer. Just remember to eat fats only until you feel full and not overdo on your fats. Look for plant-based fats and try to stay away from seed and vegetable oils because these are almost always highly processed.

4. Don't ever forget to keep track of your carbs. Most vegan diets are naturally high in carbs because they are plant-based, and plants are full of carbs. It is possible to stick to your daily carb limit, but you will need to be careful and plan your meal selections wisely. You will not be able to achieve and maintain a state of ketosis, which is absolutely necessary for the keto diet to work if you do not maintain strict control of your intake of carbs.

5. The quality of the protein that you eat matters. It is essential that you eat enough of the right kind of protein because the quality of it matters as much as the quantity. The nine essential amino acids that your body can't create are easily found in animal food, which you will not be eating. You can, however, combine different kinds of plant foods to get the amounts of the essential amino acids that your body needs. Start your meal plans with the recommended amount of protein but plan to add in a few more grams if needed. Proteins that come from plants are not digested as easily as proteins that come from animals. So people who follow a vegan diet may need more protein than people who do not follow a vegan diet. If you add in more protein, begin with just a few grams at a time and add more slowly. Excess protein, like excess sugar, is easily converted to glucose in your body, and it can throw you out of ketosis. You will also need to eat protein throughout the day and not all in one meal because your body functions best on a steady stream of small amounts of protein.

So, what foods are you allowed to eat on the keto vegan diet? There are many. You will need to mix and match different foods in order to create meal plans that are nutrient-dense and still fall in the guidelines needed to keep your body in ketosis.

Fruits

Fruit is the candy that comes from nature. It is the sweet treat that will keep you going when you need a quick pick-me-up. If you choose the right fruits, then you will still be able to enjoy fruit on the keto diet. The keto diet will help you to lose weight because it forces your body to burn fat for energy instead of carbs. This is why you will need to limit your intake of carbs when you are on the vegan keto diet. When you are counting the carbohydrate count in any food, remember to take out the amount of fiber that is in the food because the fiber does not count when you are counting your carbs for the day. So if one medium banana has twenty-seven grams of carbs and three grams of fiber, its net carb count is twenty-four.

$$27 - 3 = 24$$

These are still too much carbs to eat on a low carb diet, so bananas will not be in your dietary plan. There are a few fruits that you will be able to eat in moderation so that you do not feel totally deprived of something sweet. All carb counts are for a three-ounce serving.

FRUIT	CARBS	VITAMINS AND MINERALS
Watermelon	6	Vitamin A, B1, B2, B6, C, folic acid
Strawberries	6	Vitamin A, B1, B2, B6, C, folic

		acid
Cantaloupe	7	Vitamin A, B1, B2, B6, C, folic acid
Coconut (meat)	6	Vitamin A, B1, B2, B6, C, folic acid
Honeydew	7	Vitamin A, B1, B2, B6, C, folic acid
Raspberries	5	Vitamin A, B1, B2, B6, C, folic acid
Blackberries	4	Vitamin A, B1, B2, B6, C, folic acid
Blueberries	4	Vitamin A, B1, B2, B6, C, folic acid
Plum	7	Vitamin A, B1, B2, B6, C, folic acid
Lemon	6	Vitamin A, B1, B2, B6, C, folic acid
Lime	6	Vitamin A, B1, B2, B6, C, folic acid

On the keto vegan diet, the list of fruits that you are allowed to eat is much shorter than the list of vegetables that you are allowed to eat. This is because the carb count of most fruits makes them too high in carbs to be beneficial to you on the keto vegan diet. Fruits are naturally full of fruit sugar, which is a carb. Look at the situation like this: If you are consuming just twenty grams of carbs each day, then you could either eat three ounces each of strawberries, watermelon, and cantaloupe or you could eat three ounces each of broccoli, tomato, zucchini, avocado, cucumber, spinach, and green beans.

Vegetables

There are many more veggies allowed on the vegan keto diet than there are fruits, for one simple reason: veggies are not full of sugar like fruits are. Many different vegetables are allowed on the vegan keto diet, so you will find plenty of variety even if you do not like all of them. Try to eat as many different veggies as possible because this will give you variety in your diet and will make it easier for you to eat a well-balanced diet. And while you are deciding which veggies you want to eat, be sure to look at the vitamins and minerals that each one provides so you can ensure that you are getting a proper mix of the nutrients that you need. The following carb counts for these veggies are-based on a three-ounce serving, with a list of the vitamins and minerals that each one will provide you.

VEGETABLE	CARBS	VITAMINS AND MINERALS
Green beans	4	Vitamin C and folacin
Brussel Sprouts	5	Vitamin A, C, K, folate, potassium, manganese
Yellow bell peppers	5	Vitamin C
Red bell peppers	4	Vitamin C
Green bell peppers	3	Vitamin C
Broccoli	4	Vitamin A, C, K, manganese, folate, potassium
Kale	3	Copper, calcium, potassium
Cauliflower	3	Vitamin C
Zucchini	3	Vitamin A, C, K, folic acid
Cabbage	3	Vitamin C
Eggplant	3	Manganese
Tomato	3	Vitamin C
Asparagus	2	Vitamin K, thiamin, riboflavin, selenium
Cucumber	3	Vitamin A, C, K, potassium, manganese, magnesium
Avocado	2	Potassium
Lettuce (all types)	2	Vitamin A, C, potassium, magnesium, iron

Spinach	1	Vitamin A and K
Mushrooms	1	Potassium
Garlic (one clove)	1	Vitamin B6, C, selenium, manganese, calcium, iron
Radishes	2	Vitamin C and folacin
Onions	5	Vitamin C, B6, magnesium, calcium, iron
Artichokes	4	Vitamin C, K, folacin
Celery	1	Vitamin A, K, potassium, folate
Arugula	1	Vitamin C, K, folacin
Swiss chard	4	Vitamin A, C, E, magnesium, iron, phosphorus

Nuts, Seeds, and Nut Butters

Nuts, seeds, and nut butters are an absolute must on the keto vegan diet. First, they are strictly plant-based food. Second, while you do need to watch the carb counts of most nuts, they are packed full of protein and fat, the kind of fat that is good for you. Some nuts are lower in carbs, and some are higher. But they are an excellent food item to include in your low carb meal plans. They are loaded with antioxidants, vitamins, and minerals. And they assist with all of the good health benefits that you are trying to enjoy from the keto vegan diet, such as lower blood pressure and cholesterol, weight loss, and better cardiovascular health. You can buy them shelled or unshelled, roasted, raw, plain, seasoned, unsalted, or salted. Nut butters are full of fiber, healthy fats, vitamins and minerals, and protein. This table shows nuts, seeds, and nut butters that you should include in your meal plans and the benefits they bring to you.

NUT OR SEED	CARBS	VITAMINS AND MINERALS	PROTEIN
Brazil nuts	4	Vitamin E, magnesium, selenium	4 grams
Pecan	4	Vitamin E, magnesium	3 grams
Pumpkin seeds	5	Vitamin A, K, potassium, phosphorus	8 grams
Macadamia nuts	5	Vitamin E, magnesium	2 grams
Walnuts	7	Vitamin E, magnesium	4 grams

Peanuts	7	Vitamin E, magnesium	4 grams
Hazelnuts	7	Vitamin E, magnesium	6 grams
Pine nuts	8	Vitamin A, K, folate, potassium	7 grams
Chia seeds	8	Iron, calcium, copper, magnesium	10 grams
Almonds	10	Vitamin E, magnesium	6 grams
Hemp seeds	5	Vitamin B6, potassium, magnesium	9 grams
Cashews	9	Vitamin E, magnesium	5 grams

NUT BUTTERS	CARBS	VITAMINS AND MINERALS	PROTEIN
Almond butter	3	Vitamin E, Omega-3, calcium, magnesium	7 grams
Hazelnut butter	12	Vitamin E, copper, manganese	4 grams
Macadamia nut b.	4	Vitamin B6, iron, thiamine, manganese	2 grams
Peanut butter	6	Antioxidants	8 grams
Pecan butter	6	Vitamin A, B, E, potassium, magnesium	4 grams
Sunflower Seed b.	4	Vitamin E, antioxidants	6 grams
Tahini	3	Vitamin B, E, iron, magnesium, calcium	3 grams

Walnut butter	6	Omega-3, antioxidants	8 grams
Soy Nut Butter	8	All essential amino acids	9 grams

Other Food Items

When you are cooking meals for the keto vegan diet, you will need to look for good sources of fat because you will not be getting fat from animal sources. The best place to look for these healthy fats is in the oils that you use. Stock your pantry with as many different oils as you can, because each will bring a different taste to your recipes. You can choose from walnut oil, hazelnut oil, coconut oil, macadamia nut oil, almond oil, olive oil, and avocado oil. There may be times when you need coconut flour, almond flour, coconut milk in the can, baking soda, nutritional yeast, and baking powder. You might also want to keep a supply of pickles, olives, apple cider vinegar, tofu, tempeh, seitan, and any kind of sprout you can buy. When buying any processed food, remember to read the food labels.

It is not difficult to assemble good tasting and healthy keto vegan meal plans. Just watch your carb counts and make sure you are getting the right mix of nutrients for your body, and you will be just fine.

Chapter 5: Micros and Macros

On most diets, people count calories to achieve a weight loss goal. If a person weighs this much, and they want to weigh less, then they will need to consume fewer calories and possibly add in some form of exercise. While exercise is always a good thing for anyone, whether you are dieting or not, on the keto vegan diet, it is not really necessary to count your calories. The foods you will be eating do not have enough calories, most of the time, to add any substantial weight gain to your body. The difference to that would be the nuts, seeds, and nut butters you eat or if you eat any processed vegan food like meats and cheeses.

The important things for you to focus on are your micros and your macros. Micronutrients (micros) are the vitamins, minerals, and other nutrients that your food will provide to you and that your body needs to stay healthy. Macronutrients (macros) are nothing more than the three types of foods that you will eat, fats, proteins, and carbs.

Macros

Counting your macros can help you to build muscle mass or lose weight. This method is dependent on you keeping track of the types of foods that you eat and the calories in them so that you will consume a specific number of macros. To be able to count and control them successfully, you really need to know what they are, what they do for you, and how they affect your diet.

Proteins are necessary for certain processes in your body to work the right way. This includes secreting certain enzymes and hormones, building and rebuilding tissues, cell interaction, and the proper functioning of your immune system. Proteins provide four calories per each gram.

Fats are needed by your body to help it maintain a proper temperature as well as absorb nutrients from the foods that you eat and produce necessary hormones. Fat is the most calorie-dense of the three nutrients with nine calories per gram.

Carbs are now the least of your macros, but you will still be consuming some, mostly in the form of vegetables and a few fruits. Since carbs are metabolized into glucose in your body, you obviously need to limit them. Carbs have four calories per gram, just like protein does.

If you have decided to count your calories, then you will need to find the proper ratio of micronutrients. The typical macro breakdown for the keto vegan diet is sixty-five percent fat, thirty-five percent protein, and five percent carbs. You can adjust these amounts as you need to but keep the carb count low. Don't let the fat count get too much lower because you will need fats to give you energy. You can track your macros on any one of the numerous online counters, or you can simply make columns in a spiral notebook and write them down every day.

So if you are calculating your macros for a two thousand calorie diet and you want to eat sixty-five percent fat, thirty-five percent protein, and five percent carbs you calculations would look like this:

Fat – nine calories per gram – 65% x 2000 = 1300 / 9 = 144 grams per day

Protein – four calories per gram – 35% x 2000 = 700 / 4 = 175 grams per day

Carbs – four calories per gram – 5% x 2000 = 100 / 4 = 25 grams per day

So each day, you will consume one hundred forty-four grams of fat, one hundred seventy-five grams of protein, and only twenty-five grams of carbs. One benefit to counting macros is that it might make you more aware of the food that you are eating. If you compare the calories in a bowl of oatmeal that is topped with pumpkin seeds and berries to a bowl of processed sugary cereal, you will find that the calorie count is similar, but the macros are vastly different. The bowl of sugary cereal is almost all carbs, where the other choice has carbs with healthy fats and proteins.

And if you have a specific goal in mind for your body, it might benefit you to count your macros. If you want to increase your athletic ability in any way, then counting your macros can help you to reach your goal, whether that goal is building long, lean muscles or adding bulk to certain areas. You might feel a bit confused when you first begin to count your macros and that is natural. Just follow the steps and calculations will be easy. The first step is to set your goal for intake of calories and then to determine how many of each macro you need to consume each day. Log your food intake and your macros, and this system will soon be natural and simple for you.

Micros

There are six specific nutrients that the human body needs on a regular basis to sustain a healthy life. Those nutrients are water, fat, protein, carbs, minerals, and vitamins. Water is just that – water. Fat, protein, and carbs are macronutrients, the big categories. No less important are the micronutrients, the minerals, and vitamins your body uses to drive every function that your body does. It is always best, whenever possible, to get your micros from food because these are produced naturally, by nature, and they are the easiest for your body to utilize.

Micros are needed to balance the levels of hormones in your body. They also drive the function of your immune system and help your body keep its bones and muscles strong. The cells of the bones and muscles are constantly dying and replenishing, and they can't do this without the proper nutrients. Certain foods supply certain vitamins and nutrients. Knowing what these micros are will help you to make the right choices for the foods in your diet so that your meals provide the proper mix of micros to help you reach your goal. Here are the minerals and vitamins that you will need to get from your food.

Vitamin A – To maintain healthy eyes, teeth, and skin

Vitamin B1 – Thiamine, to fuel energy, combats stress, and supports your digestion

Vitamin B2 – Riboflavin, supports antioxidant function and fuels energy

Vitamin B3 – Niacin, reduces inflammation and improves circulation

Vitamin B5 – Pantothenic acid, necessary for the production of hormones and red blood cells

Vitamin B6 – Pyridoxine, regulates wake and sleep cycles and moods

Vitamin B7 – Biotin, supports the digestive system and skin and nerve function

Vitamin B9 – Folate, fights congenital disabilities in pregnant women

Vitamin B12 – Helps prevent anemia, Alzheimer's disease, and memory loss

Vitamin C – Helps prevent scurvy which is characterized by slow wound healing and bleeding gums

Vitamin D – Secosteroids, assists your body in processing magnesium, iron, and calcium

Vitamin E – Tocopherols, protects the body from the damage caused by free radicals

Vitamin K – Keeps bones healthy and helps blood to clot properly

Zinc – Reduces the risk of catching an infectious disease and boosts the immune system

Potassium – Helps to prevent kidney stones, cardiovascular disease, and osteoporosis

Phosphorus – Keeps bones and teeth healthy

Omega-3 Fatty Acids – A necessary anti-inflammatory

Magnesium – Helps the body metabolize fats and carbs

Iron – Responsible for carrying oxygen throughout the body

Choline – Helps the liver function properly

Calcium – Besides keeping your bones strong it also helps with muscle contraction and the health of your blood vessels

Antioxidants – Helps with every bodily function and also assists in maintaining the health of the body

Since Vitamin B12 can only be found in animal products, it may be impossible for you to get this vitamin from your diet no matter how healthy it is. But you should be able to achieve and maintain a good supply of all the nutrients that your body needs if you make every effort to consume a rich and varied vegan diet.

Chapter 6: Vegan Keto Recipes

Here are some recipes to get you started on your vegan keto journey. After you have tried these, you will be better equipped to start creating your own delicious concoctions.

Breakfast Recipes

1. Curried Tofu Scramble

Press tofu thirty min/prep ten min/cook twenty min/ serves four

Ingredients:

Scramble

- Mushrooms, button, sliced, six ounces
- Onion, diced, one half of a medium size
- Red bell pepper, cleaned and diced, one large
- Spinach, chopped roughly, three cups
- Tofu, firm, one block
- Vegetable broth or olive oil, one tablespoon

Sauce

- Coriander, one quarter teaspoon
- Cumin, one quarter teaspoon
- Curry powder, one half teaspoon
- Garam masala, one quarter teaspoon
- Garlic powder, one quarter teaspoon
- Paprika, one quarter teaspoon
- Salt, one half teaspoon
- Turmeric, one quarter teaspoon

Method:

You will need to press and drain the block of tofu for thirty minutes before you can begin the recipe. Pressing tofu is relatively simple. Completely cover a plate with several paper towels and set the block of tofu in the middle. Cover the tofu with another layer of paper towels. Set a cutting board or another plate on top of the paper towels that are on top of the tofu and then put some heavy object on that, like cans from your pantry or a book. This will press out all of the excess water that will prevent your tofu from keeping its shape.

After you have finished pressing the tofu, put the olive oil or the vegetable broth into a hot skillet and cook the onions for five minutes. Mix in the mushrooms and the chopped red peppers and cook for another ten minutes. Then push all of the veggies into one half of the skillet and add the tofu to the other half of the skillet. Use a spoon or a spatula to break the tofu up into bite-sized or smaller pieces. Cook the tofu for five minutes. While the tofu is cooking, use a small bowl or a mug to put all of the seasoning ingredients in for the 'sauce' and mix them together well. Sprinkle this mixture over the tofu and the veggies in the skillet and then mix all of the ingredients together well. Stir in the chopped spinach and cook the mix for five more minutes and then serve hot.

Nutrition info per serving: Calories 118, eight grams carbs, eleven grams protein, four grams fat

2. Chia Breakfast Pudding

Prep three min/serves two

Ingredients:

- Almond butter, one tablespoon

- Chia seeds, four tablespoons

- Cinnamon, one teaspoon

- Coconut milk, three-fourths of one cup

- Cold coffee, three-fourths of one cup

- Vanilla extract, one tablespoon

Method:

Into a bowl or a jar, put all of the listed ingredients and mix them together very well. Cover the container and let the pudding sit in the refrigerator overnight. This kind of pudding can be made with almost any item you can think of. Experiment with many different varieties of mixes and find the ones you like the best.

Nutrition info preserving: Calories 282, five grams carbs, six grams protein, twenty-four grams fat

3. Cinnamon Roll Muffins

Prep five min/cook fifteen min/makes twenty muffins

Ingredients:

Muffins

- Almond flour, one half cup

- Baking powder, one teaspoon

- Cinnamon, one tablespoon

- Coconut oil, one half cup

- Nut butter or seed butter, one-half cup your choice: almond, sunflower, etc.

- Pumpkin puree or unsweetened applesauce, one half cup

- Vanilla protein powder, two scoops

Glaze

- Coconut butter, one-quarter of one cup

- Lemon juice, two teaspoons

- Milk, non-dairy of choice, one-quarter of one cup

Method:

Heat the oven to 350. Set paper cups into a twelve cup muffin pan and set it off to the side. Put all of the listed dry ingredients into a large-sized mixing bowl and blend them together well. Then add in the list of wet ingredients and mix well until the batter is smooth. Pour the batter carefully into the paper muffin cups, keeping the levels of batter as even as possible. Bake the muffins in the oven for ten to fifteen minutes, then test one of the muffins by sticking a knife or a toothpick into the center. If it comes out clean, then the muffins are done. If not, then give them another one or two minutes. Leave the muffins in the pan to cool for the first five minutes, and then put them out onto a wired rack so they can finish cooling. As soon as the muffins are cool, then mix the ingredients for the glaze. Dribble the glaze over the cooled muffins and allow it to get hard, and then serve. These muffins need to be eaten within two days. If you would like to freeze them for later, use just wrap each muffin individually.

Nutrition info per one muffin: Calories 112, three grams carbs, five grams protein, nine grams fat

4. Low Carb Pancakes

Prep ten min/cook ten min/serves one

Ingredients:

- Almond butter, unsweetened, two tablespoons

- Almond milk, unsweetened, one-fourth of one cup

- Baking powder, one-half teaspoon

- Coconut flour, one tablespoon

- Coconut oil, two tablespoons

- Flax, ground, one tablespoon

- Salt, one-quarter teaspoon

*Method :*Over a medium-high heat set a large frying pan and add in the olive oil. Cream together the almond milk and the almond butter. In a different bowl, mix together all of the dry ingredients until they are well mixed. Mix the butter and milk mixture into the dry ingredients, stirring well until all of the dry ingredients are wet. Let this mixture sit and rest for five minutes so that the coconut flour and the flax can absorb the excess liquid in the mix. Spoon the mix into the hot oil to fry the pancakes; the batter should make three or four pancakes. Fry the pancakes for four to five minutes on each side. You will want to see small bubbles all over the top in the batter before you flip it over. Top the pancakes with the topping of your choice like fresh fruit, vegan butter, or sugar-free syrup.

Nutrition info per recipe: Calories 260, twenty-one grams fat, ten grams protein, five grams carbs

5. Cauliflower Hash Browns

Prep five min/cook ten min/serves six

Ingredients:

- Cauliflower, one half of one head broken into small pieces

- Chickpea flour, one-quarter of one cup

- Coconut oil, one tablespoon

- Cornstarch, one tablespoon

- Garlic powder, one half teaspoon

- Onion, one half chopped

- Salt, one half teaspoon

Method:

Heat the oven to 400. With aluminum foil or parchment paper, cover a cookie sheet. Lightly spray the covering with spray oil. Grate the cauliflower and the onion until they are finely grated. Put this mixture into a large-sized bowl. Combine in the salt, garlic powder, cornstarch, and chickpea flour and mix until the ingredients are well blended. Separate the batter into six equal-sized portions and form them into patty shapes. Set the patties on the cookie sheet and bake for twenty minutes. Turn them over and bake for twenty more minutes.

Nutrition info per patties: Calories 144, six grams fat, six grams protein, twenty grams carbs

6. Maple Oatmeal

Prep five min/cook twenty min/serves four

Ingredients:

- Almond milk, one-third of one cup

- Chia seeds, four tablespoons

- Cinnamon, one teaspoon

- Coconut flakes, unsweetened, one-quarter of one cup

- Maple flavoring, one teaspoon

- Pecans, one half of one cup

- Sunflower seeds, unsalted, three tablespoons

- Walnuts, one half of one cup

Method: Crumble the walnuts, pecans, and sunflower seeds in a food processor. Set a large-sized pot on the stove and place the nuts into it after they have pulsed. Blend in well in the remainder of the ingredients and then turn the heat on under the pot to medium. Bring the mix just to a simmer and then let it simmer for thirty minutes while you stir often. This is needed so that the chia seeds will not stick to the bottom. Serve the hot oatmeal with a sprinkle of cinnamon if so desired.

Nutrition info per serving: Calories 374, four grams carbs, ten grams protein, thirty-five grams fat

7. Mediterranean Style Breakfast Burrito

Prep fifteen min/ cook five min/serves six

Ingredients:

- Avocado oil, two tablespoons

- Black olives, sliced, three tablespoons

- Nutritional yeast, one half of one cup

- Refried beans, canned, three-fourths of one cup

- Salsa for garnish

- Spinach, two cups, washed and dried

- Tomatoes, chopped, three tablespoons

- Tortillas, ten-inch size, low carb, six

Method:

Cook the spinach, black olives, and tomatoes in a large skillet in the avocado oil for five minutes while you are stirring constantly. Put two tablespoons of the refried beans on each of the tortillas and spread it over the tortillas, going just to one inch from the edge. Divide the veggie mixture evenly over the tortillas. Roll each one up by folding the sides in and then rolling the tortilla. Put them back in the skillet with the leftover olive oil and fry the rolled burritos for three minutes on each side. Serve them with the salsa if desired.

Nutrition info per burrito: Calories 252, nineteen grams carbs, fourteen grams protein, eleven grams fat

8. Vegan Bagels

Prep ten min/cook forty min/makes six

Ingredients:

- Baking powder, one teaspoon

- Ground flaxseed, one half of one cup

- Psyllium husks, one-quarter of one cup

- Salt, one quarter teaspoon

- Tahini, one half of one cup

- Water, one cup

Method: Heat the oven to 375. Cover a cookie sheet by wrapping it with aluminum foil or laying parchment paper over it. Blend well together in a medium-sized mixing bowl, the baking powder, salt, ground flax seeds, and the psyllium husks and stir together until they are combined well. In another smaller bowl, cream together the tahini and the water. Pour the mixed together wet ingredients into the mixed together dry ingredients in the larger bowl and mix them well until they form the dough. Divide the ball of dough into six lumps of dough that are all about the same size. With your hands gently flatten all of the lumps until they are rounded into patties and about one-quarter inch thick. Lay each of the patties on the cookie sheet and use a small circular item to cut a small round shape out of the middle of each one. Bake the bagels for forty to forty-five minutes or until they turn a golden brown. Let the bagels cool before you eat them, and top them any way you would like to or eat them plain. Nutrition info per bagel: Calories 209, sixteen grams fat, two grams carbs, seven grams protein

9. Quiche Cups

Prep ten min/cook thirty min/makes twelve cups

Ingredients:

- Cornstarch, one tablespoon

- Dijon mustard, two tablespoons

- Garlic powder, two teaspoons

- Lemon juice, one tablespoon

- Nutritional yeast, one half of one cup

- Spinach, frozen, thawed, four cups

- Tofu, extra firm, one block (fourteen ounces)

- Tomato paste, one tablespoon

- Water, three tablespoons

Method: Heat the oven to 350. Put paper cups in all of the cups of a twelve cup muffin pan and set it to the side. Toss together all of the listed ingredients into a blender except for the spinach and blend them on high until the mixture is creamy and smooth. Put the spinach into a large bowl and then pour the mix from the blender into the bowl. Stir the liquid mix together with the spinach and then divide this mix into the twelve muffin cup papers, making them as even as possible. Bake the muffins for thirty to thirty-five minutes or until just the edges are turning slightly brown.

Nutrition info per muffin: Calories 57, two grams fat, three grams carbs, six grams protein

10. Chocolate Cinnamon Smoothie

Prep five min/serves one

Ingredients:

- Avocado, one half of one

- Cacao powder, unsweetened, two teaspoons

- Cinnamon, ground, one tablespoon

- Coconut milk, three-fourths of one cup

- Coconut oil, one teaspoon

- Vanilla extract, one quarter teaspoon

Method:

Blend together well all of the ingredients that are listed and drink immediately.

Nutrition info per smoothie: Calories 300, thirty grams fat, fourteen grams carbs, three grams protein

Lunch Recipes

1. Mushroom Sandwich with Greens

Prep forty minutes/cook forty-five min/serves four

Ingredients:

- Arugula or spinach, two cups, cleaned and chopped and cooked as desired

- Black pepper, one half teaspoon

- Coconut cream, one-quarter of one cup

- Eggplant, four slices

- Garlic, minced, one tablespoon

- Lemon juice, one teaspoon

- Olive oil, one tablespoon

- Portobello mushroom caps, four large with gills removed

- Salt, one half teaspoon

- Tomato, one large, sliced into four slices

Method:

Mix well together in a small bowl the coconut cream, garlic, and lemon juice. Brush the olive oil over the eggplant slices and the mushroom caps and fry them in a large-sized skillet for five minutes on each side. Use one teaspoon of the coconut cream mixture to spread over the inside of the mushroom caps and then lay a slice of eggplant on top of each mushroom cap. Add a slice of tomato on top of each slice of eggplant. If there is any leftover coconut cream mixture, then use it to drizzle over the stacked mushroom caps and the cooked greens. Serve these while they are hot.

Nutrition info per serving: Calories 289, fifteen grams carbs, ten grams protein, eleven grams fat

2. Grilled Eggplant Rollups

Prep five min/cook eight min/serves eight

Ingredients:

- Basil, dried, two tablespoons

- Black pepper, one teaspoon

- Eggplant, one medium-sized

- Olive oil, two tablespoons

- Tomato, one large

Method:

Peel the eggplant and cut off both ends so that they are flat. Slice the eggplant from one end to the other in slices that are about one-eighth of an inch thick. Slice the tomato into eight thin slices and set them to the side. Carefully brush the olive oil on the slices of eggplant using a pastry brush and then grill the slices in a hot skillet for three minutes on each side. When all of the slices have been grilled on both sides, then lay a slice of tomato on each of the slices of eggplant. Sprinkle the black pepper and the basil over the tomato slices and then roll up the slices of eggplant with the tomatoes inside.

Nutrition per one roll: Calories 59, four grams carbs, three grams protein, three grams fat

3. Greek Salad

Prep fifteen min/serves six

Ingredients:

Salad

- Black olives, one half of one cup slice

- Cherry tomatoes, one cup slice

- Cucumber, one peeled, quarter and slice

- Nutritional yeast, one half of one cup

- Olive oil, two tablespoons

- Parsley, fresh, one half of one cup chop

- Red onion, one small thin-slice

- Romaine lettuce, four cups chop

- Salt, one quarter teaspoon

- Yellow bell pepper, cleaned and diced

Dressing

- Balsamic vinegar, two tablespoons

- Black pepper, one half teaspoon

- Garlic, minced, one tablespoon

- Olive oil, one-third of one cup

- Oregano, one quarter teaspoon

- Salt, one quarter teaspoon

Method:

In a small bowl or large jar mix all of the ingredients that are listed for the dressing and blend until they are well mixed. Put this to the side while you prepare the salad. In a larger sized bowl, add in the bell pepper, onion, parsley, tomatoes, olives, and cucumber. Toss these ingredients gently but well until they are all mixed together well. Divide the salad evenly among six bowls. Spoon a portion of the dressing onto each bowl and then sprinkle on the nutritional yeast.

Nutrition info per serving: Calories 294, eleven grams carbs, fifteen grams protein, twelve grams fat

4. Peppers Stuffed with Vegetables

Prep thirty min/serves six

Ingredients:

- Balsamic vinegar, two tablespoons

- Black pepper, one half teaspoon

- Celery, washed and diced, four stalks

- Cherry tomatoes, cut in quarters, one cup

- Cucumber, one half, peeled and diced

- Dijon mustard, three tablespoons

- Green bell peppers, three, cleaned and cut in half across the middle

- Parsley, fresh, one-quarter of one cup chopped

- Salt, one quarter teaspoon

- Scallions, one bunch, cleaned and sliced

- Soy yogurt, one half of one cup

Method:

In a large-sized mixing bowl, blend together the mustard, soy yogurt, balsamic vinegar, mustard, pepper, and salt. Drop in the cucumbers, scallions, tomatoes, and the celery and mix all of these together gently but thoroughly. Use a smaller sized spoon to put this mixture into the halves of the peppers. Nutrition info per pepper half: Calories 117, nine grams carbs, seven grams protein, three grams fat

5. Spicy Lentil Soup

Prep twenty min/cook fifty min/serves eight

Ingredients:

- Black pepper, one teaspoon
- Celery, fine chop, one half of one cup
- Cilantro, chopped, one half of one cup
- Cinnamon, one tablespoon
- Ginger, two tablespoons minced
- Lentils, dry, one half of one cup
- Olive oil, three tablespoons
- Paprika, one tablespoon
- Parsley, fresh, chopped, one half of one cup
- Salt, one half teaspoon
- Tomato, two large, cleaned and diced
- Vegetable broth, seven cups
- Yellow onion, one chopped fine

Method:

Set a large skillet over medium heat on the stove and add in the olive oil. Then fry the ginger, onion, garlic, and celery for ten minutes while you stir the mix frequently. Mix in the paprika, salt, pepper, turmeric, and the cinnamon and cook the mix for five more minutes. Pour in the vegetable broth and add in the tomatoes, cilantro, and the lentils. Mix this all together well and let the soup simmer over a lowered heat for thirty minutes.

In small amounts like in this soup, lentils are very low in carbs.

Nutrition info per two cups of soup: Calories 240, fifteen grams carbs, fourteen grams protein, eight grams fat

6. Tomato and Red Pepper Soup

Prep fifteen min/cook forty-five min/serves four

Ingredients:

- Black pepper, one half teaspoon

- Cayenne pepper, one quarter teaspoon

- Garlic, minced, one tablespoon

- Italian seasoning, one half teaspoon

- Olive oil, three tablespoons

- Onion, one medium, cut in quarters

- Paprika, ground, one half teaspoon

- Parsley, fresh, chop, one-quarter of one cup

- Red bell peppers, two, seeded and diced

- Salt, one half teaspoon

- Tomato paste, two tablespoons

- Tomato, three, clean and dice

- Vegetable Broth, vegetable, two cups

Method:

Heat the oven to 425. In a large-sized mixing bowl, blend together the garlic, onion, red pepper, and tomatoes with olive oil, salt, and pepper. Mix the veggies well so that all of them are well coated with the oil. With aluminum foil or parchment paper covers a cookie sheet. Spread out the veggies onto the cookie sheet and bake them for forty-five minutes. Place a large pot over medium-high heat on the stove and pour in the vegetable broth. Let it heat until it is boiling and then turn the heat to a lower heat and pour in the vegetables after they are roasted. Stir this all together well and let it cook for another ten minutes.

Nutrition info per one cup: Calories 150, eleven grams carbs, four grams protein, four grams fat

7. Niçoise Salad

Prep forty minutes/serves four

Ingredients:

Salad

- Basil leaves, chopped fine, one half of one cup
- Bibb lettuce, one large head
- Black olives, pitted, one half of one cup
- Black pepper, one teaspoon
- Grape tomatoes, one cup
- Green beans, French style, four ounces
- Olive oil, one tablespoon
- Red onion, thin-sliced, one half of one cup
- Salt, one half teaspoon
- Tofu, extra firm, eight ounces crumbled into small pieces

Dressing

- Black pepper, one half teaspoon
- Garlic, one clove minced

- Lemon juice, two tablespoons

- Olive oil, three tablespoons

- Salt, one quarter teaspoon

- Water, one tablespoon

Method:

Put all of the ingredients that are listed for the salad dressing into a small bowl or a large jar and blend them together until they are well mixed. Put the dressing mix in the refrigerator while you are preparing the salad mix. Boil in hot water the green beans for five minutes and then drain them well. Divide the Bibb lettuce evenly between four plates. Divide the green beans, onions, black olives, tomatoes, and tofu. Serve the chilled dressing on the side.

Nutrition per serving: Calories 350, twelve grams carbs, twenty-two grams protein, eleven grams fat

8. Cilantro Lime Coleslaw

Prep ten min/serves five

Ingredients:

- Avocados, two

- Cilantro leaves, fresh, one half of one cup

- Coleslaw, ready-made in a bag, fourteen ounces

- Garlic, minced, two tablespoons

- Lime juice, two tablespoons

- Salt, one half teaspoon

- Water, one-quarter of one cup

Method:

Chop the cilantro leaves until they are finely chopped and mix them with the minced garlic. Peel the avocados after wiping them off and remove the pits and discard. Mash the pulp of the avocados and cream it together with the lime juice and the water. Add in the minced garlic and cilantro. This blend needs to be smooth and creamy. Add in the coleslaw mix and toss it with the dressing mix gently but completely. Put the coleslaw in the refrigerator for one hour before serving it.

Nutrition info per serving: Calories 119, three grams carbs, three grams protein, nine grams fat

9. Zucchini Noodles with Avocado Sauce

Prep ten min/serves two

Ingredients:

- Avocado, one

- Basil, one and one fourth cup

- Cherry tomatoes, twelve sliced in thirds

- Lemon juice, two tablespoons

- Pine nuts, four tablespoons

- Water, one-third of one cup

- Zucchini, one

Method:

Wipe off the skin of the zucchini and then peel it. Then either use a spiralizer cutter or a vegetable peeler to cut the zucchini into spiral noodles that look like spaghetti. Put all of the rest of the ingredients into a blender except for the cherry tomatoes. Blend all of these ingredients together until they make a smooth sauce. Put the zucchini noodles into a large bowl and pour the creamy sauce from the blender over them. Mix the noodles together well but gently. When they are fully mixed toss in the cherry tomato slices and then serve immediately. You can also save this salad for serving later, but don't keep it for more than two days.

Nutrition info per serving: Calories 313, twenty-six grams fat, nineteen grams carbs, seven grams fiber

10. Cauliflower Fried Rice

Prep five min/cook ten min/serves four

Ingredients:

- Carrot, one-quarter of one cup chopped fine

- Garlic, minced, two tablespoons

- Green onion, one-quarter of one cup

- Olive oil, two tablespoons

- Riced cauliflower, twelve ounces frozen or fresh

- Sesame oil, toasted, one teaspoon

- Soy sauce, two tablespoons

- Tofu, firm, pressed and chopped into pellet sized pieces, four ounces

Method:

Into a large skillet over medium-high heat pour the olive oil. Add in the chopped carrots and the riced cauliflower. Cook these together for five minutes, stirring them sometimes. Into this mix, you will add the minced garlic and the chopped green onions and stir them in well. Cook all of this mix for another three minutes. Now stir in the small pellets of tofu and mix them in well with the other ingredients. Cook the mix with the tofu for five minutes, just to warm the tofu. Pour in the sesame oil and the soy sauce, stir these in quickly, and then serve.

Nutrition info per serving: Calories 114, six grams carbs, four grams protein, eight grams fat

11. Roast Baby Eggplant

Prep twenty min/cook forty-five min/serves four

Ingredients:

To Cook

- Baby eggplant, eight

- Black pepper, one teaspoon

- Olive oil, two tablespoons

- Salt, one teaspoon

For Serving

- Salt, one teaspoon

- Black pepper, one teaspoon

- Olive oil, two tablespoons

- Nutritional yeast, one half of one cup

Method:

Heat the oven to 350. Wipe off the outside of the eggplant and cut each of them in half from one end to the other. Cover completely a cookie sheet with parchment paper or aluminum foil. Lay each of the eggplants halves on the covered cookie sheet with the inside facing up. Rub olive oil on the inside part of each baby eggplant and then sprinkle them with the salt and pepper. Bake the baby eggplants in the preheated oven for forty-five minutes. The flesh will become soft and slightly brown. While the eggplant halves are cooking mix together the olive oil with the salt and pepper. Just before serving, the eggplant halves drizzle them with the seasoned olive oil mix and sprinkle on the nutritional yeast. Nutrition per half an eggplant: Calories 44, one gram carbs, one gram protein, four grams fat

12. Sweet Potato and Squash Patties

Prep fifteen min/coon ten min/serves two

Ingredients:

- Applesauce, unsweetened, one half cup

- Avocado oil, two tablespoons

- Black pepper, one teaspoon

- Cumin, ground, one quarter teaspoon

- Garlic powder, one half teaspoon

- Parsley, dried, one quarter teaspoon

- Salt, one half teaspoon

- Squash, shredded, one cup

- Sweet potato, shredded, one cup

Method: Blend well the squash, sweet potato, and applesauce together in a large mixing bowl. Stir in the parsley, garlic powder, cumin, salt, and pepper and mix these seasonings thoroughly. Set a large-sized skillet on the stove over medium-high heat and pour in the olive oil. While it is warming divide the mixture in the bowl into four equal-sized portions. When the olive oil is hot, set each portion in the skillet in the hot oil and press the portions down until they are one half to one inch thick. Let the portions fry for five minutes before gently turning them over. Fry them on the other side for five minutes and serve them while they are hot.

Nutrition info per patty: Calories 112, six grams carbs, three grams protein, nine grams fat

13. Cranberry Chickpea Salad

Prep twenty min/serves four

Ingredients:

- Black pepper, one teaspoon

- Cherry tomatoes, red, one cup cut in halves

- Cherry tomatoes, yellow, one cup cut in halves

- Chickpeas, one cup drained and rinsed

- Cranberries, one cup washed and sliced in halves

- Cucumber, chopped, one cup

- Lemon juice, two tablespoons

- Olive oil, two tablespoons

- Parsley, fresh, chopped, one-quarter of one cup

- Red onion, sliced thin, one half of one cup

- Salt, one half teaspoon

Method:

Toss the onion, cranberries, chickpeas, cucumber, and tomatoes in a medium-sized mixing bowl. In a separate smaller bowl, blend well together with the lemon juice, olive oil, parsley, salt, and pepper. Pour the bowl of wet ingredients over the bowl of dry ingredients and mix them together gently but very well. Nutrition info preserving: Calories 145, nine grams carbs, four grams protein, eight grams fat

14. Thai Soup

Prep ten min/cook fifteen min/serves four

Ingredients:

- Bell pepper, red, one-half cut in julienne strips

- Cilantro, one half of one cup chopped

- Coconut milk, one fourteen ounce can

- Garlic, minced, two tablespoons

- Ginger, ground, one tablespoon

- Lime juice, two tablespoons

- Mushrooms, three sliced thinly

- Onion, red, one-half cut in julienne strips

- Tamari, one tablespoon

- Thai chili, finely chopped, one half of one

- Tofu, firm, pressed and cubed, ten ounces

- Vegetable broth, two cups

Method:

Set a large cooking pot or a Dutch oven on the stovetop and turn on the heat to medium-high. Pour in the vegetable broth and the coconut milk and mix them together well. Stir in the mushrooms, garlic, ground ginger, Thai chili, red bell pepper, and onion and mix all of these ingredients together well. Right when the liquid begins to boil, keep stirring often and let the soup cook for five minutes. Now add in the tofu and let the mix cook for another five minutes. Take the pot of soup off of the heat and stir in well the cilantro, lime juice, and the tamari. Mix these in well and then serve the soup.

Nutrition info per serving: Calories 339, eight grams carbs, fifteen grams protein, twenty-seven grams fat

15. Butternut Squash with Mustard Vinaigrette

Prep twenty min/cook fifty min/serves six

Ingredients:

- Apple cider vinegar, one tablespoon

- Black pepper, one teaspoon

- Dry mustard, one tablespoon

- Olive oil, four tablespoons

- Parsley, chopped, one-quarter of one cup

- Salt, one half teaspoon

- Shallots, eight, cut into wedges

- Squash, three small butternuts peeled, seeded and cut in half

Method: Heat the oven to 375. In a large mixing bowl, add together the shallots and the squash. Season them with the olive oil, salt, and pepper and toss them gently to get all of the pieces well covered. Cover completely a large cookie sheet with aluminum foil or parchment paper. Lay out the shallots and the squash on the cookie sheet in a single layer and bake them for fifty minutes. While the vegetables are in the oven baking cream together the apple cider vinegar, dry mustard, and the parsley to make the vinaigrette for the veggies. When they have finished baking, then lay the veggies on a serving plate and drizzle over them with the vinaigrette. Nutrition info per serving: Calories 135, eleven grams carbs, one gram protein, ten grams fat

Dinner Recipes

1. Zucchini Lasagna

Prep twenty min/cook one hour/serves nine

Ingredients:

For the Ricotta

- Basil, finely chopped fresh, one half of one cup

- Black pepper, one teaspoon

- Lemon juice, two tablespoons

- Nutritional yeast, two tablespoons

- Olive oil, one tablespoon

- Oregano, dried, two teaspoons

- Salt, one half teaspoon

- Tofu, extra firm, one sixteen ounce block drained and pressed for ten minutes

- Water, one half of one cup

Other Ingredients

- Marinara sauce, one twenty eight-ounce jar

- Zucchini, three medium sliced paper-thin from end to end

Method:

Heat the oven to 375. Crumble the block of tofu and put it in a blender or large mixing bowl. Add to the tofu the olive oil, lemon juice, water, salt, pepper, oregano, basil, and the nutritional yeast. Continue blending all of these ingredients together until the mixture looks like a creamy paste. Use spray oil to grease a nine by thirteen-inch baking dish. Pour only one cup of the marinara sauce into the baking dish and use a spoon or a spatula to spread it around. Cover the marinara sauce with thin slices of the zucchini. Use a teaspoon to drop small amounts of the tofu ricotta mix over the zucchini and gently spread it around until the strips of zucchini are almost all covered. Dribble some more of the marinara sauce over the tofu ricotta mix and then lay on another layer of the slices of zucchini. Keep making more layers until all of the filling and all of the slices of zucchini have been used up. The two layers that are on the top should be marinara sauce on top of zucchini. Cover this dish with aluminum foil and put it in the preheated oven. Bake the zucchini lasagna for forty-five minutes and then remove the foil covering and bake it for another fifteen minutes. Cut it into nine squares the moment you take it out of the oven and sprinkle the top with more of the chopped fresh parsley.

Nutrition info per square: Calories 338, thirty-four grams fat, ten grams carbs, five grams protein

2. Tofu in Tomatoes

Prep five min/cook twenty min/serves two

Ingredients:

- Black pepper, one teaspoon

- Chili powder, one quarter teaspoon

- Garlic, minced, two tablespoons

- Olive oil, one tablespoon

- Oregano, one teaspoon

- Rosemary, one teaspoon

- Salt, one teaspoon

- Thyme, one quarter teaspoon

- Tofu, one block medium, unpressed, cut into rounds one-half-inch thick

- Tomatoes, one fifteen ounce can, diced

Method:

 Pour in the olive oil to a large skillet on the stove over medium-high heat. When it is hot, stir in the minced garlic and fry it for two minutes. Blend in the thyme, rosemary, oregano, pepper, salt, chili powder, and tomatoes. Mix all of these ingredients together well. After they are well-mixed turn down the heat under the skillet so the mixture can simmer. Let it cook at a simmer for five minutes. Lay the rounded slices of tofu into the tomato mixture and then let the mix simmer undisturbed for fifteen minutes, or until the sauce is somewhat thick and the tofu has begun to get soft.

Nutrition info per serving: Calories 284, sixteen grams carbs, twenty grams protein, ten grams fat

3. Cauliflower Rice with Mushrooms

Prep twenty min/cook thirty min/serves six

Ingredients:

- Black pepper, one teaspoon

- Cauliflower, riced, four cups

- Garlic, minced, six cloves

- Mushrooms, button, one cup sliced thin

- Nutritional yeast, one half of one cup

- Olive oil, two tablespoons + two tablespoons

- Onion, one small, well diced

- Parsley, fresh, chopped, two tablespoons

- Salt, one half teaspoon

- Shallot, one large, minced

- Vegetable broth, two cups divided

Method:

On the stove over medium-high set a large skillet and pour in two tablespoons of the olive oil. Add the garlic, shallot, and onion to the hot olive oil and fry them together for five minutes. Pour into this mix the mushrooms and one cup of the vegetable broth and mix this together well. Cook all of this for five more minutes. Now stir in the other cup of the vegetable broth along with the riced cauliflower. Stir the mixture often while you cook it for ten more minutes. Add in the pepper, salt, and parsley and stir them into the mix. Let the mix simmer in the skillet for fifteen to twenty minutes while the mixture thickens.

Nutrition info per serving: Calories 297, seven grams carbs, seven grams protein, twenty-six grams fat

4. Spaghetti Squash Greek Style

Prep forty min/cook thirty min/serves two

Ingredients:

- Avocado oil, two tablespoons

- Cherry tomatoes, eight-cut in three slices

- Chickpeas, one-third of one cup, drained and rinsed

- Garlic, minced, one tablespoon

- Marjoram, dried, one teaspoon

- Nutritional yeast, two tablespoons

- Onion, red, one-quarter of one cup sliced thinly

- Rosemary, dried, one teaspoon

- Salt, one half teaspoon

- Spaghetti squash, one large

- Spinach, fresh or frozen chopped finely, one cup

- Thyme, dried, one half teaspoon

Method:

Heat the oven to 400. Wipe off the outside skin of the spaghetti squash and then cut it in half from one end to the other end. Scoop out the seeds using a spoon. Oil lightly the insides of the squash with one tablespoon of the avocado oil. Cover completely a cookie sheet with parchment paper or aluminum foil. Lay the spaghetti squash on the cookie sheet with the inside facing down. Use a fork to poke three or four holes into the skin of the squash. Bake the squash for thirty minutes in the heated oven. Once the squash has cooked, remove it from the oven and use the tines of a fork to scrape the cooked flesh out of the spaghetti squash; it will come out in strings that look like spaghetti. Put it in a bowl and set it off to the side. Set a large skillet on a medium heat and add in the remaining tablespoon of avocado oil. Toss in the onion and the garlic and cook them for five minutes, stirring occasionally. Then blend in the thyme, rosemary, marjoram, tomatoes, and chickpeas and cook this mix for five more minutes. Mix in the salt, spinach, and spaghetti squash and stir constantly while you cook this for five more minutes. Sprinkle over the top of the nutritional yeast and serve while the dish is hot.

Nutrition info per serving: Calories 272, fourteen grams carbs, eleven grams protein, ten grams fat

5. Stuffed Portobello Mushrooms

Prep twenty five min/cook fifteen min/serves four

Ingredients:

- Balsamic vinegar, two teaspoons

- Basil, ground, one tablespoon

- Black pepper, one-half teaspoon and one half teaspoon

- Cherry tomatoes, one cup cut in half

- Garlic, minced, one tablespoon

- Olive oil, three tablespoons divided

- Portobello mushrooms, four, remove the gills and stems*

- Salt, one-quarter teaspoon and one quarter teaspoon

- Thyme, one teaspoon

- Turmeric, one tablespoon

Method:

Heat the oven to 400. In a small-sized mixing bowl, mix together the garlic, one-quarter teaspoon of salt, and one-half teaspoon of pepper with two tablespoons of the olive oil. Use this mixture to coat the caps of the mushrooms well on both sides. Cover completely a cookie sheet with parchment paper or aluminum foil. Lay the mushroom caps on the cookie sheet and bake them for ten minutes.

While the mushrooms are baking mix together in a small bowl, the remainder of the olive oil, salt, and pepper along with the thyme, turmeric, basil, and tomatoes. When the mushrooms have finished baking, then remove them from the oven and fill the insides with this mixture. Drizzle the balsamic vinegar over the filled mushroom caps before serving.

You can purchase just the Portobello mushroom caps if you prefer. If you want to remove the caps yourself, just take a spoon to scrape away the gills from the underneath of the caps after you twist off the stems. After the gills are removed, then the underside of the caps will be smooth.

Nutrition info per mushroom cap: Calories 186, six grams carbs, sixteen grams fat, six grams protein

6. Creamy Curry Noodles

Prep ten min/cook ten min/serves four

Ingredients:

Noodle Bowl

- Bell pepper, red, one cleaned and diced

- Carrots, two, peeled and cut in julienne strips

- Cauliflower, one half of one head chopped small

- Cilantro, fresh, chopped small, one half of one cup

- Kale, two cups packed

- Zucchini noodles, one sixteen ounce pack

Creamy Curry Sauce

- Apple cider vinegar, two tablespoons

- Avocado oil, two tablespoons

- Black pepper, one half teaspoon

- Coriander, ground, one and one half teaspoons

- Cumin, ground, one teaspoon

- Curry powder, two teaspoons

- Ginger, ground, one quarter teaspoon

- Salt, one teaspoon

- Tahini, one-quarter of one cup

- Turmeric, ground, one teaspoon

- Water, one-quarter of one cup

Method:

Into a large bowl, place the zucchini noodles, and cover them with two cups of boiling water. Set this bowl to the side. After five minutes, drain off the water and then put the noodles back into the bowl. After prepping the veggies toss the cilantro, bell pepper, carrots, and cauliflower into the noodles. Lay the kale leaves onto four serving plates. Put together all of the ingredients for the Curry Sauce and either cream it together well in a high-speed blender or mix it in a mixing bowl. Pour the creamy sauce over the ingredients in the large mixing bowl and toss everything together gently but very well. Divide the noodle mix over the kale leaves on the plates and serve.

Nutrition info per serving: Calories 192, fifteen grams fat, sixteen grams carbs, five grams protein

7. Portobello Mushroom Tacos

Prep twenty min/cook ten min/yields six tacos

Ingredients:

Tacos

- Cumin, ground, one teaspoon

- Green collard leaves, six

- Harissa, mild or spicy, one-quarter of one cup

- Olive oil, three tablespoons divided

- Onion powder, one teaspoon

- Portobello mushrooms, one pound

Guacamole

- Avocado, two medium-sized

- Cilantro, chopped fine, one tablespoon

- Lime juice, two tablespoons

- Red onion, chopped fine, two tablespoons

- Salt, one half teaspoon

- Tomatoes, chopped fine, two tablespoons

Method:

Pull the stems off of the Portobello mushrooms and use a spoon to remove the gills from the underneath side. Rinse off the mushroom caps and pat them dry. In a small-sized bowl cream together the onion powder, cumin, harissa, and one and one-half tablespoons of the olive oil until all ingredients are creamy and smooth. Use a spatula or a knife to completely cover the underside of each of the mushroom caps with this mixture, making sure to cover the edges too. Let them sit and marinate for fifteen minutes. Mix together the guacamole while you are letting the mushrooms marinade. After wiping off, the avocados cut them in half and use a spoon to scoop out the flesh. Put the flesh into a medium-sized bowl. Blend in the red onion, lime juice, salt, cilantro, and chopped tomatoes. Rinse and dry the leaves of the collard greens and cut off the tough stems. When the mushrooms have finished marinating, put the remainder of the olive oil in a large skillet over medium-high heat and let it get hot. Put the mushroom caps in the hot oil and fry them for three minutes on each side. Take the mushrooms from the oil and lay them on a paper-towel-lined plate. Let them rest for five minutes before you slice them. Lay a few slices of mushroom cap in a collard leaf. Top the slices with the guacamole and enjoy.

Nutrition info per two collards: Calories 405, thirty-five grams fat, sixteen grams carbs, ten grams protein

8. Sushi Bowl

Prep five min/serves one

Ingredients:

Bowl

- Cauliflower rice, cooked, one half of one cup

- Cucumber, one-quarter of one cup cubed

- Salad greens, one cup packed

- Tofu, firm, pressed, four ounces

Toppings

- Avocado, one-quarter of one sliced

- Parsley, one tablespoon

- Sesame seeds, one teaspoon

Method:

Place all of the ingredients for the bowl into a medium-sized mixing bowl and toss all of the ingredients gently but carefully. Mix together in a separate small bowl all of the ingredients listed for the toppings. Place the contents of the medium-sized bowl into a serving bowl and then top them with the toppings ingredients.

Nutrition info per bowl: Calories 289, twenty-one grams fat, six grams carbs, sixteen grams protein

9. Egg Roll in a Bowl

Prep five min/cook fifteen min/serves two

Ingredients:

- Black pepper, one teaspoon

- Cabbage, four cups shredded

- Carrots, two shredded to make one cup

- Green onions, chopped, one half of one cup for garnish

- Mushrooms, one cup sliced

- Olive oil, one tablespoon

- Onion, red, one half sliced thin

- Salt, one quarter teaspoon

- Sesame oil, one teaspoon

- Sesame seeds, one-quarter of one cup for garnish

- Tamari, two tablespoons

Method: On the stove, set a large-sized skillet over medium-high heat and warm up the olive oil. Fry the celery, carrots, and onions for five minutes. Pour in the tamari, salt, pepper, mushrooms, and shredded cabbage. Stir all of these ingredients together well. Turn the heat down under the pan to low and let this mixture simmer for fifteen minutes. Stir in the sesame oil for one minute and then take the pan off of the heat. Serve with the chopped green onions and the sesame seeds for garnish. Nutrition info per serving: Calories 178, twelve grams carbs, six grams protein, nine grams fat

10. Zucchini Ravioli

Prep twenty five min/cook thirty five min/serves six

Ingredients:

Zucchini

- Basil, fresh, one cup

- Black pepper, one half teaspoon

- Cashews, raw, one cup

- Garlic, minced, three tablespoons

- Salt, one half teaspoon

- Spinach, fresh, one cup

- Walnuts, one cup

- Water, one cup

- Zucchini, four medium-sized

Pine Nut Hemp Parmesan

- Hemp seeds, one-quarter of one cup

- Pine nuts, one-quarter of one cup

- Salt, one quarter teaspoon

Topping

- Marinara sauce, one large jar

Method:

Heat the oven to 350. Mix the ingredients for the pine nut hemp parmesan in a medium-sized bowl and grind them together with a pestle or use a food processor until they are nice and crumbly. Wash and peel the zucchini and slice them in very thin strips from one end to another. You should be able to make thirteen to fifteen strips from each zucchini. Lay the slices of zucchini out on a paper towel, not overlapping and sprinkle them with a bit of salt. Mix together the water, basil, spinach, salt, pepper, garlic, walnuts, and cashews until all of these ingredients are mixed well. Grind all of the ingredients well with a pestle or in a food processor until they are almost pureed but still rather chunky. The salted zucchini strips will have water drawn out of them by the salt. Wipe it off with a paper towel. Place two of the slices of zucchini on a plate in an 'X' shape. Drop a spoonful of the ricotta mixture in the middle of the X. Take the ends of the strips and bring them all to the middle to make a small pocket. Put each of the ricotta-filled pockets into a nine by thirteen-inch baking pan. When you have assembled all of the ravioli and placed them in the baking pan, cover them with the marinara sauce. Sprinkle the pine nut hemp parmesan on top of the marinara. Bake the casserole for forty to forty-five minutes and let it stand for ten minutes before serving. This recipe will make thirty raviolis, and one serving is five ravioli.

Nutrition info per five raviolis: Calories 360, thirty grams fat, fifteen grams carbs, twelve grams protein

11. Indian Roasted Vegetables

Prep ten min/cook twenty min/serves four

Ingredients:

Veggies

- Cauliflower, one cup in small pieces

- Green beans, three-fourths of one cup

- Mushrooms, sliced one half of one cup

Masala Seasoning

- Black pepper, one half teaspoon

- Chili powder, ground, one half teaspoon

- Garam masala, one quarter teaspoon

- Garlic, minced, one tablespoon

- Ginger, ground, two teaspoons

- Olive oil, two tablespoons

- Salt, one half teaspoon

- Tomato puree, one half of one cup

- Turmeric, one quarter teaspoon

Garnish

- Cilantro, chopped, one-quarter of one cup

- Green onion, diced, one half of one cup

Method:

Heat the oven to 400. Set the oven rack in the middle of the oven. Cover a cookie sheet. If the veggies have not been chopped, then chop them now. In a medium-sized bowl, blend well together with the garlic, ginger, chili powder, garam masala, salt, pepper, and the tomato puree until all of the ingredients are mixed together well. Mix in the olive oil. Drop the chopped veggies into this mix and stir them around in the mix until all of the veggies are covered well. Lay the veggies out on the cookie sheet in a single layer. Put the cookie sheet in the oven and roast the veggies for twenty to thirty minutes or until the veggies are cooked the way you like them.

Nutrition info per serving: Calories 105, seven grams fat, ten grams carbs, three grams protein

12. Cauliflower Pie

Prep thirty min/cook thirty min/serves four

Ingredients:

- Balsamic vinegar, one-quarter of one cup

- Black pepper, one teaspoon

- Carrots, two medium-sized peeled and diced fine

- Cauliflower, one head

- Celery, one stalk washed and diced fine

- Dijon mustard, one tablespoon

- Garlic, minced, three tablespoons

- Mushrooms, diced small, one cup

- Nutmeg, ground, one teaspoon

- Nutritional yeast, three tablespoons

- Olive oil, two tablespoons

- Olive oil, two tablespoons + two tablespoons

- Onion, one medium-sized diced finely

- Salt, one half teaspoon

- Thyme, dried, one teaspoon

- Tomato paste, one tablespoon

- Vegetable broth, one cup

Method:

Heat the oven to 400. Chop up the cauliflower into small pieces and put them into a large saucepan on the stove. Cover the cauliflower with water and turn on the heat to medium-high. Bring the water to a boil and cook for eight to ten minutes or until the pieces of cauliflower are very tender. Drain the water off and put the cauliflower into a medium-sized bowl and set it to the side. Set a large-sized skillet on the stove over medium-high heat. Warm the olive oil and pour in the celery, carrots, and onion. Cook these for five minutes, stirring occasionally. Pour in the diced mushroom and cook for another five minutes. Blend in the balsamic vinegar and the tomato paste. Cook for two minutes and then stir in the vegetable broth. Turn the heat of the burner down to low and cook this mixture at a simmer for ten minutes, or at least until around half of the liquid has been absorbed. While this mix is cooking use a potato masher to mash the cooked cauliflower. When the cauliflower is well mashed, then adds in the other two tablespoons of olive oil with the mustard, pepper, nutmeg, thyme, salt, and nutritional yeast. Pour the veggie mix into a square nine by nine-inch casserole dish and top the veggie mix with the mashed cauliflower mixture. Bake the casserole for twenty minutes.

Nutrition info per serving: Calories 400, fifteen grams carbs, eleven grams protein, fifteen grams fat

13. Korean Beef Bowl

Prep fifteen min/cook ten min/serves two

Ingredients:

- Broccoli, cooked, one cup

- Cauliflower rice, two cups

- Mushrooms, cooked, one half of one cup

- Scallions, chopped, one half cup

- Sesame oil, two tablespoons

- Sesame seeds, two teaspoons

- Tamari, low carb, one tablespoon

- Tofu, firm, pressed and drained, baked, one cup

Method:

Put the sesame oil into a large skillet over medium-high heat. Pour into the skillet the cooked mushrooms, cooked broccoli, cooked cauliflower, and baked tofu. Stir all of the ingredients often until they are well mixed and heated thoroughly about fifteen minutes. Add in the tamari and the sesame seeds and mix them in well. Divide the mix between two bowls and top with the chopped scallions and serve.

Nutrition info per bowl: Calories 247, thirteen grams fat, nine grams carbs, eighteen grams protein

14. Veggie Salad Bowl

Prep thirty min/cook twenty min/serves four

Ingredients:

Salad

- Asparagus, one large bunch

- Avocado, one cubed

- Bell pepper, red, one medium

- Celery, two stalks diced

- Lettuce, mixed leaves, two cups packed

- Olive oil, two tablespoons

- Parsley leaves, one half of one cup packed

- Purple cabbage, shredded, one half cup

- Salt, one half teaspoon

- Spinach, fresh, two cups packed

- Walnuts, one-quarter of one cup

- Zucchini, one small

Vinaigrette

- Apple cider vinegar, two tablespoons

- Black pepper, one teaspoon

- Dijon mustard, two teaspoons

- Olive oil, three tablespoons

- Salt, one half teaspoon

Method:

Heat the oven to 400. Peel off the skin of the zucchini and cut off the ends. Cut the zucchini in half the long way and then slice it into diagonal pieces about one-half-inch thick. Wash and clean the bell pepper and cut it into slices. Clean the asparagus. Put all of the veggies into a medium-sized bowl and cover them with the salt and the olive oil. Mix the veggies together well until all of the pieces are well coated. Wrap a cookie sheet with aluminum foil or parchment paper and put the veggies on it in a single layer. Bake the veggies in the heated oven for twenty minutes. While the veggies are baking mix together all of the ingredients for the dressing in a small bowl. When the veggies are done baking, divide them between four bowls and drizzle the mixed dressing over all of them. Serve immediately.

Nutrition info per bowl: Calories 313, five grams carbs, five grams protein, thirty grams fat

15. Roast Brussel Sprouts with Garlic and Red Pepper

Prep ten min/cook twenty min/serves four

Ingredients:

- Black pepper, one teaspoon

- Brussel sprouts, two pounds

- Garlic, minced, two tablespoons

- Olive oil, four tablespoons divided

- Red pepper, crushed, one half teaspoon

- Salt, one half teaspoon

Method:

Heat the oven to 500. Trim off the bottom stem from the Brussel sprouts. Put them into a mixing bowl of medium-sized along with two tablespoons of the olive oil and the salt and pepper. Toss the sprouts gently until all are well covered. Spread the oiled Brussel sprouts out onto a cookie sheet and cover them over with a sheet of foil. Bake them for ten minutes and take off the sheet of foil. Bake the Brussel sprouts for another ten minutes. While they are in the oven, put the remaining two tablespoons of olive oil into a medium-sized skillet and fry the minced garlic and the crushed red pepper together for three minutes. When the Brussel sprouts have finished cooking, toss them together with the fried garlic and red peppers and serve.

Nutrition info per serving: Calories 195, fifteen grams fat, eight grams carbs, six grams protein

Desserts

Even on the keto vegan diet, you will still be able to enjoy dessert sometimes. Just try one of these five recipes and see how delicious a dessert that is good for you can be.

1. Spiced Chocolate

Prep ten min/makes eighteen pieces

Ingredients:

- Black pepper, one eighth teaspoon

- Cacao butter, melted, one-quarter of one cup

- Chili powder, one half teaspoon

- Cinnamon, one teaspoon

- Cocoa powder, one half of one cup

- Nutmeg, one quarter teaspoon

- Sale, one eighth teaspoon

- Stevia, liquid, twenty-five drops

- Vanilla extract, one half teaspoon

Method:

Blend together the cocoa powder, salt, pepper, nutmeg, cinnamon, and chili powder until the ingredients are mixed well. Put the cacao butter in a bowl that is safe to use in the microwave and heat it on high for thirty seconds, and then stir it well. Keep heating it for thirty seconds and then stirring it until it is all melted. Cream together the stevia and the vanilla extract with the melted cacao butter. Stir the cacao butter mix into the mixed dry ingredients and keep stirring until the mixture is creamy and smooth. Use spray oil to grease an eight by eight-inch square pan and pour the candy mixture into the pan, smoothing it out by using a spatula or the back of a large spoon. Let the chocolate candy rest at room temperature until it is firm.

Nutrition info per one piece: Calories 40, three grams fat, six grams carbs, one gram protein

2. Coconut Bars

Prep three min/cook three min/makes twenty bars (servings)

Ingredients:

- Coconut flakes, unsweetened, three cups

- Coconut oil, one cup melted

- Maple syrup, one-fourth of one cup

Method:

Put parchment paper into an eight by eight-inch pan or dish and set it off to the side. Put the shredded coconut into a large-sized mixing bowl. Blend in the maple syrup and the coconut oil. Mix all of this together well until it becomes a thick batter. If it is stiff or not creamy enough, add some water a few drops at a time until it becomes the correct consistency. Pour this coconut cookie bar mix into the parchment paper-lined dish and smooth it out. Place the dish in the refrigerator until the bars have become firm, then slice and eat.

Nutrition info per bar: Calories 108, eleven grams fat, two grams carbs, two grams protein

3. Blueberry Cake

Prep ten min/cook thirty-five min/makes twelve pieces (servings)

Ingredients:

- Almond flour, two cups

- Applesauce, unsweetened, one-fourth of one cup

- Baking soda, one teaspoon

- Blueberries, one cup

- Cinnamon, one tablespoon

- Coconut flour, one-fourth of one cup

- Coconut oil, one-fourth of one cup

- Maple syrup, one-fourth of one cup

- Vanilla extract, one teaspoon

Method:

Heat the oven to 350. Use spray oil to grease an eight by eight-inch baking pan and set it off to the side. Stir together in a large-sized mixing bowl, the almond flour, baking soda, coconut flour, and cinnamon until all of the ingredients are blended together well. In a different medium-sized bowl cream together the maple syrup, coconut oil, vanilla extract, and the applesauce until all ingredients are well mixed and creamy. Slowly pour the wet ingredients into the bowl of the dry ingredients, stirring well the entire time that you are pouring. Keep mixing gently until all of the dry and wet ingredients are well mixed together. Pour in the cup of blueberries and gently fold them into the batter, mixing just until they are all mixed in. Pour the mixed batter into the greased eight by eight-inch pan and bake the cake in the hot oven for forty minutes. Leave the cake in the pan for ten minutes to cool before removing it to a serving plate. Serve the cake warm or cooled.

Nutrition info per slice: Calories 135, seven grams carbs, eight grams protein, eleven grams fat

4. Three Ingredient Flourless Cookies

Prep three min/cook ten min/makes twelve cookies

Ingredients:

- Almond butter, one cup

- Applesauce, unsweetened, three-fourths of one cup

- Chia seeds, ground, four tablespoons

Method:

Heat the oven to 350. Wrap a cookie sheet with aluminum foil or cover it with parchment paper. In a large-sized mixing bowl cream, all of the ingredients together until they are creamy and smooth. Make the cookie dough into small one inch sized balls and place them on the cookie sheet three inches apart. Press each one slightly flat with a fork or your fingers. Bake the cookies for just eight to ten minutes.

Nutrition info per cookie: Calories 101, three grams carbs, five grams protein, nine grams fat

5. Apple Pie Muffins

Prep five min/cook fifteen min/makes twelve muffins

Ingredients:

Muffins

- Almond butter, one half of one cup

- Almond flour, one half of one cup

- Applesauce, unsweetened, one half of one cup

- Baking powder, one teaspoon

- Cinnamon, one teaspoon

- Cloves, ground, one half teaspoon

- Coconut oil, melted, one half of one cup

- Nutmeg, one teaspoon

- Vanilla protein powder, two scoops

Glaze

- Coconut butter, one half of one cup

- Coconut milk, one-fourth of one cup

- Lemon juice, one tablespoon

Method:

Heat the oven to 350. Put muffin papers in the cups of a twelve cup muffin pan and set it to the side. In a small bowl cream together the applesauce, coconut oil, and the almond butter. In a larger sized bowl mix together the vanilla protein powder, nutmeg, ground cloves, cinnamon, baking powder, and almond flour. Mix together in the larger bowl the dry and wet ingredients and mix them all together very well. Divide this batter evenly in the twelve muffin cups. Bake the muffins for ten to fifteen minutes or until a knife inserted in one comes out clean. Let the cooked muffins cool in the muffin pan for ten minutes. After ten minutes, you can set them on a wire rack to finish cooling. While the muffins are cooling, mix up the ingredients for the glaze and put it on when the muffins are completely cooled, just before serving.

Nutrition info per muffin: Calories 86, five grams fat, five grams carbs, six grams protein.

Snacks

While snacks are not usually recommended on a keto diet, there are times when you need a little something to keep you happy until the next meal or for times when you are exerting more energy than you normally do.

1. Avocado Cucumber Bites

Ingredients:

- Avocado, one large, peeled and pitted

- Chives, chopped, one-quarter of one cup

- Cucumber, one medium-sized

- Lime juice, one half teaspoon

Method:

Peel the cucumber if you want to and then slice it into slices that are about one half of one inch thick. Lay the slices on a plate. Mash the peeled avocado and then mix in the lime juice. Set one teaspoon of mashed avocado on top of each of the cucumber slices. Sprinkle the chopped chives on the top of the avocado.

2. Soy Yogurt Spinach Artichoke Dip

Ingredients:

- Artichoke hearts, one can fourteen-ounce size drained and chopped small

- Garlic, minced, two teaspoons

- Nutritional yeast, one half of one cup

- Soy yogurt, plain, one cup

- Spinach, thawed from frozen, one ten-ounce package

Method:

Heat the oven to 350. Use spray oil to grease an eight by eight-inch baking pan. Squeeze the thawed spinach in between layers of paper towels until all of the water is drained out. Mix together all of these ingredients and pour them into the oiled baking dish. Bake the dip for thirty minutes and serve it hot with vegan chips.

Or Try One of These Low Carb Alternatives

- Bell pepper slices, one cup is eighteen calories, zero grams fat, two grams carbs, one gram protein

- Broccoli florets, one cup is forty calories, zero grams fat, three grams carbs, three grams protein

- Cauliflower florets, one cup is twenty-five calories, zero grams fat, two grams carbs, two grams protein

- Celery, two stalks are twenty calories, zero grams fat, two grams carbs, one gram protein

- Cherry tomatoes, one cup is twenty-seven calories, zero grams fat, four grams carbs, one gram protein

- Cucumber slices; one cup is sixteen calories, zero grams fat, three grams carbs, and one gram protein

- Olives, three-fourths of one cup is one hundred fifteen calories, eleven grams fat, three grams carbs, one gram protein

- Radish slices, one cup is nineteen calories, zero grams fat, two grams carbs, one gram protein

Chapter 7: One Week Meal Plan

Since people who eat a vegan diet stay away from animal products and people who follow a keto diet trade their carbs in for fat, it would seem as though trying to do both the keto diet and the vegan diet at the same time would be counterproductive. While it is a bit challenging to merge the two, it is possible to do so.

One thing that will help you on your diet journey is to look for plant-based foods that are low in carbs but high in fat. On a vegan keto diet, seeds, nuts, and avocado will be one of the staples of your diet. There are certain food items you should always try to include in your meal planning, such as:

- Any low carb vegetables, such as leafy greens, broccoli, zucchini, mushrooms, and cauliflower

- Seeds and nuts

- Any fruit that is low carb or high in fat content such as berries or avocados

- Versatile vegan proteins like seitan, tofu, and tempeh

- Oils made from plants like avocado oil, coconut oil, and olive oil

- Vegan milk products that are high in fat, like soy yogurt, vegan cheese, unsweetened coconut milk, and coconut cream

Avocados are versatile enough to use in almost any recipe, and they also work well sliced on the side of anything. When looking at nuts, try to find the ones that are highest in fat and lowest in carbs, like almonds or macadamia nuts. Nuts are also great to carry along as a quick snack or as part of a meal on the go. Protein is important in your diet, so you will want to include seeds, nuts, and tofu. Some whole grains and beans may be eaten but only in moderation because they tend to be higher in carbs than you will want on your diet. Quinoa is a great choice because it is low in carbs and high in protein, but keep your serving sizes small. You want to avoid starchy vegetables like corn, peas, and beans. Replace these veggies with low starch options like squash, mushrooms, eggplant, cucumbers, asparagus, broccoli, and artichokes.

There are four tried, and true facts that will help you to get your vegan keto diet started off right and will also help you to stay on the right course.

- Eat the widest variety of foods possible. It is important for you to make every effort to keep your diet choices as varied as possible since the vegan keto diet is naturally very restrictive. Choose raspberries, blackberries, blueberries, strawberries, and avocado for your fruits. Your veggie options will be the non-starchy ones. Fill your menus with portions of seeds and nuts like macadamia nuts, hemp seeds, and pumpkin seeds. Look for full-fat tempeh and tofu for protein choices. You will also want to look for full-fat vegan dairy products like vegan cream cheese and cashew cheese. Round out your menu options with cauliflower pizza

crusts, zucchini or shirataki noodles, and vegan Alfredo
sauce.

- Don't forget to add the oil. Oil is a vital source of
  energy, especially when your body has entered the
  state of ketosis. Use oils in any way that you can think
  of. Drizzle oils across your veggies and salads. Cook
  with a variety of plant-based oils, like avocado oil,
  coconut oil, and olive oil. Look for oils that are high in
  polyunsaturated and monounsaturated fats, which
  include macadamia oil, flaxseed oil, avocado oil, and
  coconut oil.

- Always keep chia seeds available in your kitchen.
  These are very low in carbs and very high in fiber.
  These little seeds are versatile enough to be used in
  many different dishes. They easily absorb the flavors of
  the foods, herbs, and spices they are mixed with. And
  chia seeds are loaded with omega-3s and antioxidants.
  They also contain magnesium, phosphorus, calcium,
  manganese, fat, fiber, protein, potassium, zinc, and
  vitamins B1, 2, and 3. These little seeds are
  powerhouses that are easy to use and make great
  breakfast and snack foods.

- Learn to love the coconut. This plant-based food is low
  in carbs and high in fat. Choose from full-fat options
  like unsweetened coconut, coconut cream, and coconut
  milk. Also, look for choices like cheese made from
  coconut and yogurts made from coconut. Coconut is
  very flavorful, and using the cream version in your
  soups and curries will make them taste even better.
  Coconut is also full of nutrients that your body needs,
  like fiber, iron, selenium, copper, zinc, magnesium, and
  vitamin B6. It is cholesterol-free and low in sodium.

When you are planning your vegan keto menu options, you will need to choose foods-based on getting the proper number of grams from the three macros, fats, proteins, and carbs. The amounts of each macro that you eat on a daily basis are determined by the weight that you want to maintain. Here are the breakdowns for five different daily total calorie counts for each macro. This table is for seventy percent fat, twenty-five percent protein, and five percent carbs.

DAILY TOTAL CALORIE COUNT	FATS GRAMS	PROTEIN GRAMS	CARBS GRAMS
2000	133	175	25
1800	120	158	22
1500	100	132	19
1200	80	105	15
1000	67	88	13

CARBOHYDRATES – Keep your daily carb count between twenty and forty grams. Your carb intake will consist mostly of non-starchy veggies, especially leafy greens that can be used as the basis for anything. Don't completely ignore the starchy veggies; just keep their consumption to a minimum. The key with carbs is to get as many as possible in your diet, so you will usually want to stick to the lower-carb veggies and the lower carb fruits like berries. When you are setting your carb macro intake there are a few things you will want to consider:

- When you are just beginning the vegan keto diet, especially if your diet has been high in carbs for a long time, you might want to start out with sixty grams of carbs per day. This level of carb intake will make it easier for your body to adjust to this new diet, especially if you currently eat a lot of grains, white flours, and white sugars.

- If you are trying to lose just a little bit of weight and improve your overall energy and mental capacity, you could be just fine consuming forty grams of carbs per day.

- If you have severe hormone imbalances, brain fog, rashes, or other skin disorders, or a great deal of weight to lose, then you will want to stick to twenty grams of carbs per day and no more.

FATS – Look for all the good sources of fat you can find when making your meal plans, especially olives, seeds, nuts, coconut, and cacao, and the milk, oil, and butter made from any of these products.

PROTEIN – Your protein will come from sprouts, leafy greens, vegetables, seeds, and nuts. It will be important for you to choose foods-based on protein content first and then look at the fat content. It is harder to get enough protein on the vegan keto diet than it is to get enough fat since fat can be added to any food simply by drizzling a bit of olive oil or coconut oil over the food.

So to get into ketosis and keep your body in the best fat-burning mode possible, remember the following:

- Stick to a strict low carb diet, but try to make sure you are getting enough daily fiber.

- Keep your intake of proteins at a moderate level. Too much protein in your body will act just like too much starch; the body will convert it to glucose.

- Fat will keep you feeling fuller and more satisfied, so make sure you are getting enough. You can live on a vegan keto diet, but you can't live on a starvation diet. Fat is the main thing that will make you feel good about the foods you are eating.

- Try to avoid snacking. Eat if you are truly hungry, but try to stay at the meal plans you have set for yourself.

So exactly what will you be eating on the vegan keto diet plan? You will be eating a lot of food that tastes good and is good for you. Here is a meal plan for one week to get you started, seven days' worth of suggestions for delicious meal options.

Day One

- *Breakfast:* Prepare a chia seed pudding with almonds and coconut or raspberries and macadamia nuts

- *Lunch:* Toss leafy salad greens in a bowl and add in some seeds (like pumpkin or hemp), non-starchy veggies like mushrooms, cucumbers, and onions; and some vegan cheese or tempeh

- *Dinner:* Make some cauliflower rice with julienne slices of bell pepper, squash, or zucchini with a small salad on the side

Day Two

- *Breakfast:* Use a vegan protein powder, any flavor, and add in some nut butter, seeds like hemp or flax, and full-fat plant-based milk like almond or coconut for a delicious smoothie

- *Lunch:* Cut a wedge of tofu into small, bite-sized chunks and toss them into a bowl of leafy greens and sliced avocado

- *Dinner:* Make a delicious stir fry with slices of bell pepper, onion, and radishes sautéed lightly in olive oil and served over riced cauliflower

Day Three

- *Breakfast:* Scramble some firm tofu with chopped spinach, button mushrooms, and vegan cheese

- *Lunch:* Leafy greens and tofu with avocado dressing, easily made by thinning mashed avocado with avocado oil or olive oil until it is the right consistency

- *Dinner:* Make a vegan lasagna with strips of eggplant or zucchini, vegan cheese, and marinara sauce

Day Four

- *Breakfast:* Any full-fat plant-based yogurt with shredded unsweetened coconut and your favorite seeds on top

- *Lunch:* Make a delicious curry dish with the appropriate spices and chopped veggies and tofu

- *Dinner:* Top a low carb tortilla or cauliflower pizza crust with marinara sauce, vegan cheese, and chopped veggies for a delicious pizza

Day Five

- *Breakfast:* Mix chia seeds with your favorite thinly sliced nuts and full-fat plant-based milk for an amazing breakfast pudding

- *Lunch:* A steaming bowl of soup made with cauliflower, broccoli, vegetables broth, and full-fat coconut cream for thickening

- *Dinner:* Chop some mushrooms into vegan Alfredo sauce or a marinara sauce and serve it on top of zucchini noodles or shirataki noodles

Day Six

- *Breakfast:* Scramble some tofu with onions and a bit of vegan cheese and serve with a side of sliced avocados

- *Lunch:* Pesto and vegan cheese over zucchini noodles

- *Dinner:* Roast together slices of squash and zucchini that are drizzled with olive oil and seasoned with the spices of your choice

Day Seven

- *Breakfast:* Mix together unsweetened shredded coconut, chia seeds, ground flaxseeds, and full-fat coconut milk to make porridge

- *Lunch:* Toss chunks of low carb veggies into a soup with vegetable broth and coconut cream

- *Dinner:* Mix chunks of tofu with riced cauliflower, chopped peanuts, and chopped spinach for a great stir fry

In between meals, you might need a little snack, so choose something from the following vegan-friendly snacks:

- Berries with coconut cream

- Roasted pumpkin seeds

- Olives with vegan cheese chunks

- Sliced bell pepper with guacamole

- Chopped slivered almonds on top of plant-based yogurt

- A smoothie made with cocoa and full-fat coconut milk

- Vegan cream cheese spread on slices of cucumber

- Unsweetened coconut, seeds, and nuts made into trail mix

You have so many different choices available that you can make when planning your vegan keto menus and meals. Keep your choices low in carbs and high in fat, with a moderate amount of protein, and look for variety in the foods that you choose to eat.

Chapter 8: The Wonderful World of Herbs and Spices

You know the importance of reading the labels of any of the prepared food that you buy to supplement your vegan keto meals. You know, to look for hidden starches and sugars that could derail your dietary goals. But you also need to know and understand the importance of looking for things to add to your foods in order to make your meals more interesting. Those vital little additives are called herbs and spices. These ingredients are necessary for making your foods taste good and keeping your menu options flavorful and interesting. Cauliflower by itself is just cauliflower, and it is rather boring to the taste. But with the right herbs and spices, the simple cauliflower can take on an Indian, Spanish, or Greek flair that will liven up any meal plan. And since the menu options on a vegan keto diet do not have the added benefit of animal fat to add flavor to your food, you will need to look to herbs and spices to keep your meals fresh and lively.

While herbs and spices come from the same source, they do have some differences. An herb is derived from the leafy green part of the plant. The flower, fruit, seed, stem, bark, or root of the plant is used to make a spice. Some plants will give you both an herb and a spice, like a plant that gives you leaves that make cilantro and seeds that make coriander. Some spices will be used whole, like cloves, allspice berries, and cinnamon sticks. Whole spices keep their flavor longer than crushed herbs do, and crushed herbs keep their flavor longer than ground spices do. The more you do to an herb or a spice, the less time it will stay fresh and flavorful. It is best to buy whole varieties of your favorite spices if you have the time and the desire and then grind the little bit that you need when you are creating your meals.

You will need to use different methods when you are cooking with spices and herbs. In cooking processes, spices are always used in their driest possible form, while herbs are able to be used in their fresh form. You could pick little leaves off of a rosemary or dill plant that is sitting on your windowsill and add them into your soups. Sometimes using fresh herbs is preferable, like in salads or pesto. Dried herbs should be added into recipes at the end of the cooking time in order to keep their flavor stronger. Spices will be added usually at the beginning of the cooking process because they keep their flavor longer, and many become more flavorful by the process of cooking.

Here are some of the common herbs and spices you will want to become more familiar with in order to add flavor to the vegan keto dishes you will be creating.

ALLSPICE – this spice holds the flavor of nutmeg, cloves, and cinnamon all in one single spice.

ANISE SEED – this spice has a slight licorice taste and is especially good when paired with nuts and seeds in dishes

BASIL – this spice is a must when making tomato dishes or pesto, because of its peppery yet sweet flavor. It also mixes well with many other spices like sage, saffron, oregano, thyme, rosemary, and parsley

BAY LEAVES – these are powerful little leaves that are used for flavoring soups, just drop one in and remember to remove it and not eat it

CARAWAY SEEDS – these have a peppery taste that is especially good with lentils and cucumbers

CARDAMOM – this spice is both sweet and spicy and is great for flavoring any kind of veggie

CHILI PEPPERS – if you want to add a bit of heat and spice to your food, just add in some chopped chili peppers

CHIVES – these can be used in anything where you want to add a more subtle flavor of onion, especially in soups and salads

CILANTRO – any dish with a Spanish flair will need cilantro for flavoring

CINNAMON – this spice can be used to enhance the flavor of anything

CLOVES – these are spicy in taste yet sweet-smelling, and you will use them often in soups, and they work well with nutmeg, ginger, and cinnamon

CORIANDER – this smells a bit like an orange and gives off a warm, sweet, spicy taste

CUMIN – one of the most widely used spices, it goes well in salads and any tomato-based dish and works well with coriander

FENNEL – another spice with a mild licorice taste that is good for seasoning roast veggies

GARLIC – you can use this versatile seasoning in almost any dish, especially those with an Italian or Mediterranean flair

GINGER – this spicy-sweet and warm spice works well in either savory or sweet dishes, and you will definitely want to use it in any dish with an Asian flair like a stir fry or a noodle bowl

MACE – this spice comes from the covering on the fruit that nutmeg is made from, so it can be used in the same way that spice is used, especially in Mediterranean dishes

MARJORAM – this spice is related to oregano but is not as strong in its flavor. It has a minty flavor that is great in veggies and salads and is almost always found in Greek or Italian themed cooking

MINT – both spearmint and peppermint can be used to flavor soups and salads, and a few leaves added to boiling water makes a great afternoon tea for relaxing

NUTMEG – with a flavor somewhere between nuts and cinnamon, you will use nutmeg in soups and in veggie dishes, particularly dishes that contain cabbage, spinach, and eggplant. It is awesome in veggie ravioli

ONION – these come in many sizes and colors and can be used as much as you want to flavor any dish

OREGANO – This spice is related to marjoram, but the flavor is stronger, and it is almost always used in dishes that are-based on tomatoes. It also works well with thyme, garlic, parsley, and basil

PAPRIKA – this spice not only seasons foods but is often used as a garnish to add color to food. It has a mild sweet peppery taste

PARSLEY – this is another spice that can be used for flavor or for looks

PEPPER – this spice comes in a variety of colors that vary in their level of heat and can be used in any dish as much as you like

ROSEMARY – this is a pungently sweet spice that can be used in any veggie dish

SAGE – a pungent spice with a slightly bitter flavor that is used in salads and soups. It also tastes good in tomato-based sauces

SALT – a necessary ingredient in cooking to enhance the flavor

TARRAGON – another spice with the flavor of licorice that is good in any dish where balsamic vinegar is used

THYME – a little bit of this spice goes a long way so use it sparingly at first until you decide how much you will need in your recipes, it can be used alone or mixed with any other herb or spice

TURMERIC – This spice has a slightly gingery flavor and a beautiful yellow color; it is another one that is used for both flavor and color

Chapter 9: Keeping Vegan Keto Away From Home

When you are at home planning your meals and your weekly menus, it will be relatively easy to stick to the vegan keto diet. After all, you are the one who is making the food choices for you. But what happens when you need to venture out into the real world, the world outside of your house? It is rare when someone has the luxury of staying home all of the time. It is even rarer when someone wants to stay home all of the time. We all want to be able to eat healthy and make good food choices, but the world is out there waiting for you. You should go out and embrace it. And if you take some time to plan and make good choices, you can stick to the vegan keto diet anywhere you go.

When heading out to a restaurant, it is easier to find a vegan option or a keto option than it is to find a vegan keto option. But there are some good options for you when you are eating out. At an Asian restaurant, get something stir-fried but stay away from the noodle bowls. Any vegan-themed restaurant can help you to choose servings of non-starchy veggies, and you know that there will not be any animal products used in the making of the food. At a buffet-style restaurant, go for the veggie bar and the salad bar. Even if you choose a few items that are higher in carbs than you normally eat, you should still be within your daily allowed range for this macro. Just stay away from the creamy dressing and ask for vinegar and oil instead.

Always check out the menu online before you go if at all possible. Look for menu items like steamed veggies or salads that you can add your own items to, like cubes of tofu or nutritional yeast. Most places don't care if you do that, and the items travel really well in a small food bag. If choices are available for the vinegar and oil dressing, always choose the red wine vinegar or the apple cider vinegar and not the balsamic vinegar. Ask the server to swap out any items that are not vegan keto for items that are. And it is perfectly acceptable if you go over on your carbs at one meal every now and then. As long as most of your meals stay in the correct range of carbs, you will not be harming yourself or your diet.

Traveling and staying true to the vegan keto diet is not impossible, as long as you use a few tips to keep you on your path when you are away from home. Whether you are going on a day trip or across the country, go to the grocery store before you leave. Even if your stop is at a big-box retailer and not the fancy specialty store, you will be able to find the items you need to keep you on track. Grab some whole lemons and limes to add to your water. Coconut milk comes in a can, so it is shelf-stable and travels easily. Pick up some pre-packaged salad greens or already sliced raw veggies.

Making the right choices will allow you to stay vegan keto no matter where you are.

Chapter 10: Making Vegan Keto Work For You

There are many different reasons for embracing the vegan lifestyle. They might want to lose weight, improve their health, improve the environment, or show more love for the animal world. People embrace keto for two main reasons, and those are to lose weight and feel better. So even if you embrace the vegan lifestyle to help the environment and save the animal, you will be losing weight and feeling better, and adding the keto lifestyle to that will just increase the chances that you will soon be living an amazing new lifestyle.

While the typical keto diet relies heavily on animal fat and protein to make up the diet, the vegan keto diet does not have these benefits. You will need to pay close attention to what you are eating so that you get enough protein for your daily needs. And you might need to take a few supplements while following the vegan keto diet. While plant-based foods are loaded with minerals, vitamins, fiber, and antioxidants, they lack certain nutrients, particularly vitamin B12. Know your food and what nutrients it offers and take the time to mix your food choices to give yourself the right amount of nutrients.

Many of the proteins that you will get from plant-based foods are considered to be incomplete proteins. Proteins are made of amino acids, and there are twenty-two different ones that your body needs in order to function correctly. Of these twenty-two, your body makes thirteen, so the other nine must be found in your food choices. These are the essential amino acids, and you will need to pair your food choices so that you get all nine of them from your food.

Following the vegan keto diet will offer you a wide array of benefits to your health. The keto diet includes a high amount of fats and a low amount of carbs. The vegan diet boosts your absorption of nutrients and limits your sugar and carb intake. So the two different diets can work very well together. You will be able to improve your health by following the vegan keto diet.

You will sleep better than you ever have before. The vegan keto diet will improve your sleep. Sticking to this diet will help you to be more alert during your waking hours. That increased level of mental performance will leave you pleasantly depleted by the end of the day. You will feel ready for sleep, but you will not be exhausted from spending hours trying to keep up when you really did not have the energy to do so. Your former sugar fog will be lifted, replaced by energy and alertness that is brought on by consuming less sugar and more fat and protein that your brain needs to function properly. Reducing carbs and increasing your intake of good fats will help you to sleep better. It is all due to a hormone called adenosine, which helps your body to fall asleep and stay asleep. People who follow the vegan keto diet have higher levels of adenosine.

Your skin will be healthier and will look clearer than before.
An excess intake of carbs has been linked to many skin conditions such as eczema and acne. Along with dairy products, carbs are known to cause inflammation in your body, which can lead to unwanted allergic reactions, and most skin conditions are caused by allergic reactions. Your body reacts negatively to some of the food that you are consuming, and it reacts by creating a skin condition. Diets that are high in carbs can make acne worse and can even trigger breakouts. When you consume a diet that is high in good fats, those good fats will help your skin to feel better because it lowers the levels of inflammation in your body. And collagen, the chemical that skin depends on to stay young and healthy, is boosted by the consumption of good fats and proteins. The vegan keto diet is perfect for anyone who wants to have good skin.

You will have the energy you need to make it through the day. When your diet is full of carbs, you will frequently experience great highs and lows in your energy levels. Directly after consuming the high carb food, you will feel a great surge of energy that can drive you anywhere from a few minutes to several hours. When the sugar high wears off, you feel yourself crashing back down as the level of sugar in your blood depletes. You may even feel extreme symptoms like exhaustion or lethargy. These are due to the absence of the sugar that your body has come to depend on. When you embark on the vegan keto diet, you will consume fewer carbs and little to no sugar, so your body will no longer experience these incredible highs and lows. Your body will now get its energy from fat instead of sugar. Also, you will no longer produce too much insulin because it will not be needed since the level of blood glucose will be lowered. All of these working together will give you the constant steady levels of energy that you need to get you through the day.

The levels of hormones and hormone production in your body will be stabilized. Your body sends messages from your brain and back to your brain by using hormones. Hormones tell different parts of your body what to do and when to do it. When you are consuming a poor diet that is high in carbs, your body's production and control of hormones can be extremely chaotic. You will make hormones when you don't really need them or not make the ones you need in the amounts that you need. Ketosis will help your body to balance the production and use of hormones. When the excess sugar in your diet is eliminated, then you will produce less insulin. The good fats in your diet that help you produce ketones will help your body to produce good levels of the hormone leptin that will help to regulate your feelings of hunger. The hormone adenosine will help you to sleep longer and better. The vegan keto diet also helps the thyroid gland to better regulate the production of its hormones, which regulates every metabolic function in your body.

Your eyesight and vision will be much improved. Many of the progressive diseases that cause blindness or poor vision are directly linked to consuming a poor diet. Many people do not realize that the increased sugar levels that result in a diagnosis of Type 2 Diabetes also wreak havoc on their vision. Excess sugar levels in your blood will negatively affect your eyesight. Once the cells in the eyes begin to degenerate, they will not be able to restore themselves if your diet is poor in needed nutrients. You will be eliminating the carbs that cause high blood sugar and increasing the good fats that your eyes need to function properly.

Your stomach will feel better, and it will function better. Your stomach is full of microbiomes that help to regulate all the other functions in your body. There are trillions of tiny little microorganisms and genetic materials that reside in your stomach and intestinal tract. These bacteria play an important role in how well you are able to digest the food that you eat and how well your body absorbs and uses the nutrients that you get from your food. They also have a major role that they play in the regulation of your immune system, your metabolism, how much you weigh, your moods, and the function of your brain. If the microbiome in your gut becomes disrupted or imbalanced, it will cease to function properly. These disruptions can be caused by illness, overuse of medication, stress, carrying too much weight, and consuming a poor diet that does not give you the nutrients that you need. Even with all of the other causes of gut microbiome disruption, consuming a poor diet is the one factor that will have the biggest adverse effect on your stomach. When your diet is full of highly processed foods and artificial ingredients, this will have two important negative effects on your body. First, the microbiomes themselves will be poorly nourished. Second, the barrier that protects the microbiomes will be compromised, leaving them at risk of being damaged by outside sources. Either of these will prompt an activation of your immune system, which will then result in inflammation. The foods that you eat directly affect the health of your gut microbiomes. The vegan keto diet will allow you to eat the types of nutrients that your gut needs at the levels that are appropriate for good gut microbiome function.

You will lower your risk of developing certain types of cancer.
Even though great strides have been made in the treatment of
cancer, it is still a disease that is hard to beat in every
situation. And, unfortunately, most of the best treatments for
cancer come with negative side effects and things that will
harm your overall health. It is important to have a healthy
lifestyle and to maintain proper metabolic functioning to help
battle cancer, or even to help prevent the onset of cancer. The
sugar that you eat on a high carb diet is a food treat for cancer
cells. They grow fat and happy with all the excess sugar that
you are consuming. However, cancer cells can't live on
ketones. The ketone bodies that you make will cause cancer
cells to starve and die. And consuming a low carb diet can
help to prevent the development of many types of cancers.
The vegan keto diet will help you to be protected from
developing cancer because you will be replacing your
consumption of carbs with healthy fats.

*You will lower your potential risk of developing
cardiovascular disease.* One of the leading causes of death in
the world today is heart disease. Several different health
conditions will lead you to develop cardiovascular disease,
but most particularly obesity, poor diet, and lack of exercise.
While it is true that a diet that is high in fats is not good for
your heart, that refers to diets that are high in bad fats,
saturated fats, and trans fats. These fats are found in
processed foods and high carb foods. When you consume
good fats, you are feeding your body the good nutrients that it
needs. The vegan keto diet will give you long term benefits to
your health and particularly to your heart. The diet will help
to lower your blood pressure, triglycerides, and cholesterol, as
well as eliminating excess molecules of fat that float around in
your bloodstream and clog your arteries.

Eating this diet will help you to prevent and fight obesity and diabetes. Both obesity and diabetes are caused by excess weight, which is caused by excess consumption of carbohydrates. When you follow the vegan keto diet, you will eliminate the excess consumption of carbs, which will lower your blood sugar which will lead to less stored fat which will help you to lose weight. The vegan keto diet eliminates sugar and limits carbs, both of which lead to excess blood sugar. If you are already obese, then you will lose weight. If you already have diabetes, your blood sugar levels will become lower, which might help you to be able to get off your medication. Always follow your doctor's requirements. The vegan keto diet will also boost your metabolic rate, which will also help you to lose weight.

Your moods and your mental health will be greatly improved.
Consuming excess amounts of carbs causes significant rises
and falls in your levels of energy due to the ups and downs of
your blood sugar. This can make you feel euphorically high
one minute and devastatingly depressed the next minute. And
the excess amounts of sugar cause your brain to function
poorly. The vegan keto lifestyle will help to keep your brain
young and functioning evenly, which will help to eliminate
mood swings. When your diet is well balanced by being
moderate in the level of proteins that you consume while
keeping carbs low and good fats high, your overall brain
functioning will be improved, and your cognitive skills will
soar. The vegan keto diet also helps to eliminate certain
proteins that clump together in your brain and prevent the
proper flow of information between the brain and the body. If
you can prevent these proteins from building up in the first
place, then you may be able to prevent the development of
neuro diseases like Alzheimer's disease and Parkinson's
disease.

One of the pros of a plant-based diet is the ability to eat foods that are healthy for your body. But if you consume too many carbs, which plant-based foods are full of, you still have the risk of developing obesity-related diseases. Adding the keto factor to the vegan diet will control the amount and type of the carbs that you consume, so your consumption does not get out of control. This will leave you with plant-based healthy fats and proteins to build your diet on. You might also struggle to find enough sources of good plant-based protein, so you will need to focus on good sources like nutritional yeast and hemp seeds. Nutritional yeast is yeast that has been deactivated, which means that during processing, the yeast cells are killed off, so they become inactive. You can find it in flakes or powder and it is a great cheese substitute for vegans. The taste is a cross between cheesy and nutty.

The vegan keto diet will give you the ability to burn fat in a method that is safe and sustainable. The diet works, and you can stay on it for the rest of your life if you want to. And with all of the benefits that the vegan keto diet offers you, then there is no reason to ever resume eating a more Western type of diet. Your weight will decrease. You will definitely lower your risk of developing many of the diseases and conditions that will make your life less full. You will be eating to feed your body the proper nutrients that it needs, and this will give you all of the tools that you need to sustain a long and happy life.

Conclusion

Thank you for making it through to the end of *Vegan Keto Diet: The Ultimate Guide to Vegan Diet Plan and Prep: All You Need for Weight Loss in a Healthy Eating Regime to Reset and Energize Your Body and Mind with 50 Easy, Fast, and Delicious Recipes* by Brandon Pot. We hope that it was interesting and informative and able to provide you with all of the tools that you will need to achieve your goals no matter what they may be.

The next step is to take all the things that you learned in this book and put them to work for you. Start your journey on your vegan keto lifestyle, but making a menu plan and trying some of the recipes in this book. Don't be afraid to experiment with herbs and spices to make your food flavorful and tempting.

Finally, if you found this book useful in any way, a review on Amazon is always appreciated!

Made in the USA
Monee, IL
16 October 2020

45333880R10085